THE
RANGER
WAY

THE RANGER WAY

Living the Code on and
off the Battlefield

KRIS "TANTO" PARONTO

CENTER
STREET®

NEW YORK   NASHVILLE

Hachette Books

Hachette Book Group

1290 Avenue of the Americas, New York, NY 10104

hachettebooks.com

twitter.com/hachettebooks

First trade paperback edition: May 2018

Print book interior design by Timothy Shaner, NightandDayDesign.biz

Title page photo by Adam Bettcher for Maxim Defense—www.bettcherphoto.com

Hachette Books is a division of Hachette Book Group, Inc. The Hachette Books name and logo are trademarks of Hachette Book Group, Inc.

The publisher is not responsible for websites (or their content) that are not owned by the publisher.

The Hachette Speakers Bureau provides a wide range of authors for speaking events. To find out more, go to www.hachettespeakersbureau.com or call (866) 376-6591.

ISBN: 978-1-4789-4819-3

Printed in the United States of America

LSC-C

10 9 8 7 6 5 4 3 2 1

For JFP and RMP and for KJP, ARP, and CBP

Ranger Creed

Recognizing that I volunteered as a Ranger, fully knowing the hazards of my chosen profession, I will always endeavor to uphold the prestige, honor, and high esprit de corps of the Rangers.

Acknowledging the fact that a Ranger is a more elite soldier who arrives at the cutting edge of battle by land, sea, or air, I accept the fact that as a Ranger my country expects me to move further, faster, and fight harder than any other soldier.

Never shall I fail my comrades. I will always keep myself mentally alert, physically strong, and morally straight and I will shoulder more than my share of the task whatever it may be, one hundred percent and then some.

Gallantly will I show the world that I am a specially selected and well trained Soldier. My courtesy to superior officers, neatness of dress, and care of equipment shall set the example for others to follow.

Energetically will I meet the enemies of my country. I shall defeat them on the field of battle for I am better trained and will fight with all my might. Surrender is not a Ranger word. I will never leave a fallen comrade to fall into the hands of the enemy and under no circumstances will I ever embarrass my country.

Readily will I display the intestinal fortitude required to fight on to the Ranger objective and complete the mission, though I be the lone survivor.

CONTENTS

Chapter One

THE BATTLE FOR YOUR BEST LIFE

Battles can be beautiful. I mean that literally. It's hard to explain that to people who have never been in one. When I am looking at a firefight through night vision goggles, I can see tracers, which are rounds that burn. The color depends on the size of the round: if it's from a PKM or an AK-47, it might look green or maybe orange, and the explosions streak trails in the distance like the most spectacular light show I've ever seen. If there is heavy fire, the landscape pulses with fluorescent color. There is a snapping sound like someone cracking a whip over and over again. Those are high-velocity rounds breaking the sound barrier as they careen by my head. *Snapsnapsnap.* When mortars and rockets hit, the impact momentarily blinds my vision, and then, as it clears, I can see particles that are like charged and heated pixie dust, glowing as they rain down. I have watched all this while I felt the heat of a blazing fire as I moved toward it. My brothers and I did move toward it, striding into the chaos with absolute focus, and I was not afraid.

I was not thinking that it was the worst moment of my life. My adrenaline was surging, my world was opening up, and I might even have been thinking that this was one of the best, most important moments of my life. Because I was surrounded by my brothers, whom I trust. Because I was about to fight, which was what I had been trained to do. Every drill, every rotation, every moment of my training had prepared me for this. I was having what some scientists call a flow experience. The battle required my complete sensory involvement and the total integration of my skills and consciousness in order to complete my mission. And the mission, in battle, is always meaningful, because whatever else it might be about, lives are on the line. I am fighting for my brothers.

I am honored to have been able to fight in battle for my brothers and for my country. I was part of the CIA Annex security team that responded to the terrorist attack on the US Special Mission in Benghazi, Libya, on September 11, 2012. For more than thirteen hours that night, our team of six fought the enemy to save lives and assets. Some people are surprised when I tell them that I consider Benghazi to be one of the greatest nights of my life. That I'd go back to Benghazi in a heartbeat; you don't need to ask me twice. Just tell me where my airplane's at, I am guaranteed to be there. September 11, 2012, was a tragic night in many ways. Ambassador Christopher J. Stevens, Sean Smith, Tyrone Woods, and Glen

"Bub" Doherty died that night putting themselves in harm's way on behalf of our country. Mark "Oz" Geist and David Ubben were severely wounded. And I know that the families of the men we fought that night mourned their dead and wounded, too. It was a dangerous mess. But if I were needed, I'd be happy to go back.

People make a mistake when they think happiness is about being relaxed, kicking back over barbecue and a beer. Don't get me wrong, that can be good, and my friends will tell you that I've had plenty of days like that. A bunch of those days can be part of a good life. But the satisfaction and pride that are earned through truly optimal experiences come from being challenged, working hard, and putting your training to the test in service of a goal you care about. I'm not going to lie; sometimes that hurts while it's happening. You've got to be tough and believe that the hurt will be worth it.

Happiness comes from being tested and accomplishing your mission. That's why I'd always go back into battle. You get tested there. And you get inspired, seeing the selfless service all around you down range. I've spent the last couple years traveling around this country as a civilian, and I know it's harder to see that here at home. It's harder to see it in Washington, D.C., that's for sure. But you can create the feelings that come from optimal experience and selfless service for yourself, and you can inspire others to do the same. That's what this book is about. It's about my life and about your taking control of your own life and fighting your own battles.

But it's also about understanding that we never know what the impact of our actions is going to be. That is one of the reasons you can't ever give up.

Never quit. You're going to be hearing a lot in this book about lessons I learned while training to become an Army Ranger in the 75th Ranger Regiment. "Never quit" is a big one. You never know what the outcome of your decisions might be. Your actions might do something positive for someone else, not just you. You might even save somebody's life. Bub Doherty died a hero in Benghazi because he never gave up. Bub, along with three other GRS guys and two Delta Force operators, rented a private plane, on their own, to get to us from Tripoli, without help from Washington or the US Africa Command in Germany. We had no US air assets that night: the US outpost in Benghazi was not heavily staffed, and there were no US troops near us on alert for the anniversary of September 11, 2001. The Pentagon apparently did not know about the attack until an hour after it happened, and US assets were not in an immediate state of readiness to help. The plane that Bub's team chartered is how they got into Benghazi and how our injured got out. When Bub was flying in from Tripoli with his team, he didn't know that he was going to save lives that night or lose his own. But that plane is how my brothers Oz and Dave got the medical attention they needed when they were bleeding out in the morning. Bub's action, and his never-quit attitude, saved their lives. But I'm getting ahead of that story; I'll come back to it.

It's hard to tell the story of Benghazi. I am sincere when I say that battles can be beautiful and amazing, but that doesn't mean I like reliving the experience or talking about watching my brothers die. That might sound odd, since it seems as though talking about it is a big part of what I've been doing for the last few years. And I have a confession to make: I hate social media. I hate getting on Twitter. I hate arguing with people about the politics of our story. But I use those outlets when I have to because I can't let the story of Benghazi die. Heroes die only when their stories are forgotten. Tyrone Woods and Glen Doherty are heroes; they sacrificed everything that night. Some politicians don't see it that way. It's not necessarily political: people on both sides of the aisle have gotten things wrong. If you let the wrongs go unanswered and let the media distortions spin out of control, those guys will die all over again. I will not let that happen. And if that means I have to go on Twitter and tag CNN and MSNBC or anyone in the media when they get it wrong, I'm going to do it. When you see someone saying something that denies what you as an eyewitness know to be the truth, you must speak up. Sometimes the truth hurts. If the truth hurts your political aspirations, that's how it goes. If the truth offends you or does not seem politically correct, get over it. It's not about politics. Benghazi, for me, is about heroism, faith, sacrifice, brotherhood, and God. What the truth of our story means for you, after you hear it, might be different. But it's so important that you hear it.

And if it means I tell the story over and over, to anyone who can hear me, I'm going to keep talking. I'm more grateful than I can say for all the people who listen. If you're reading this book, then that's you, too, and I thank you. If you are a veteran reading this, I'm grateful for your service and happy that you're home. If you have ever felt misunderstood, left behind, or stuck in civilian life, I think I know what it feels like, and I hope you'll find something helpful in these pages.

* * *

Ranger training is designed to push you to your physical and mental limits and then make you hurt some more, so that you can learn how to keep working in punishing situations. Training to be a Ranger means confronting a series of physically demanding goals and tasks that increase in intensity every day. Ranger candidates are constantly scrutinized and assessed while they perform those tasks, usually in a state of sleep deprivation and hunger and frequently in unfriendly weather conditions. Sleep, food, and good weather may all be hard to come by in combat, so learning how to do without optimal conditions on the front is a key component of all special forces training. As you'll be learning in these pages, Ranger training can be flat out miserable. Being a Ranger, or training for any kind of special ops unit, is, by design, not for everyone. Using the principles of Ranger leadership and culture doesn't mean that you need to militarize your life. There is no need for most of us to train to be combat ready.

But we're all fighting our own battles, and you can use my experience and some of the principles, expectations, and techniques of Ranger training to help create your own battle rhythm and achieve victory, whatever that means to you. We all go through our own version of a battlefield. You want to do your reconnaissance, and train and prepare as hard as you can, but then you can relinquish control and let go to God. You can't control every situation in life and certainly not in combat. The action I've described on my battlefield is an extreme example, but you can experience that vividness and grace in your own life. It is all about finding your purpose, taking action, and being where you were meant to be.

You might get hurt along the way. We all hurt, and the principles behind Ranger training can be used by anyone to help you endure and overcome the hard times to achieve your goals. It doesn't matter whether your goals are physical, personal, or professional. It doesn't matter what kind of physical shape you're in, how old you are, or if you're a man or a woman. If you are willing to be honest with yourself and put in the work, you can become stronger, tougher, more disciplined, more resilient, and more confident; you can be of service to your community, be better under pressure, and, I'm betting, be happier too.

Anybody can do anything. My call sign as a GRS operator is "Tanto," and if you follow me on social media, you know that that "anybody can do anything" is a famous "Tantoism." I'm no philosopher, but if I had to drill down to my core beliefs, one of them is: you have no idea what you're capable of until you are tested. You have to allow yourself to be tested. If the circumstances of your life aren't already doing it for you, you have to push yourself and let others push you. That means that you are going to be uncomfortable and sometimes in pain, that you are sometimes going to be challenged, afraid, bone tired, and at your wits' end. You're going to want to give up if you're doing it right. But if you don't quit on yourself, you will find that you are capable of more than you ever thought you could be. Every time you don't quit, you will prime yourself to want more, to become stronger, faster, smarter, better. Other people will respond to your best self and your willingness to be challenged. And you will know the satisfaction, the gratitude, and the inner peace that come from giving life your best shot.

But first you have to define your mission, which means setting goals. Consciously setting a goal will give you concrete focus and motivation. And successful goal setting requires doing a hard, cold assessment of where you're at and what you want. Because goals that are in alignment with your purpose are the ones that you will be most likely to achieve. Goals that are in alignment with your values will keep you committed when things are tough. To set good goals, you need to understand who you are. When you have a clear vision for yourself that is in line with your values, your strengths and weaknesses, and your dreams, you'll find that pursuing the vision is just as valuable as actually achieving it.

This isn't going to be smooth sailing. But you know that already, right? You need to find the right goals and the right form of motivation, for you. That looks different for each of us and might change over time, depending on what's going on. You've got to stay flexible, humble, and curious, learn from your mistakes, and be brave.

If anything about my story helps you hang on and inspires you to make some positive change in your own life, it will make me feel even more blessed and grateful that I haven't quit. You shouldn't, either. You are capable of more than you know.

Chapter Two

BE WILLING TO SACRIFICE

*Readily will I display the intestinal fortitude required
to fight on to the Ranger objective and complete
the mission, though I be the lone survivor.*
— RANGER CREED

I f you know me as "Tanto," you probably know that I was part of the CIA Annex security team that responded to the terrorist attack on the US Special Mission in Benghazi, Libya, on September 11, 2012. Our team of six were all former military special operators, and we used everything we had to fight back against the enemy for more than thirteen hours. You probably became familiar with our ordeal from the extensive media coverage that followed or the book *13 Hours: The Inside Account of What Really Happened in Benghazi*, written by Mitchell Zuckoff and the five surviving members of our team.

But before I became known as Tanto, the private security contractor, I was Kris Paronto, Army Ranger with the 2nd Battalion, 75th Ranger Regiment. As a private security contractor, I have deployed in South America, Central America, the Middle East, and North Africa. I served four years in the US Army and an additional four years in the US Army National Guard, reaching the rank of sergeant and becoming a commissioned officer before being medically discharged in 2003. In response to the events of September 11, 2001, the US government began to use private security contractors along with full-time CIA security staffers overseas. Private security contractors are normally former military special operators like me. We were eventually designated as Global Response Staff (GRS) by the US government, and since 2004, our main task has continued to be to conduct low-profile security in high-threat environments throughout the world.

Our team of six former military men (two Navy SEALs, three Marines, and the Lone Ranger) had been hired to provide security and protect American diplomats and CIA agents working in Benghazi. On September 11, 2012, terrorists attacked the US State Department Special Mission Compound and the Annex, a nearby CIA station. Our team took action, retaking the compound and defending attacks on the Annex throughout the night, despite initially being told to stand down and warned that it was outside the scope of our duty. We fought to protect the Americans stationed there, our assets, and one another.

The public interest in those thirteen hours that our team spent in Benghazi has changed all of our lives. Some of the people who are interested in the story want to use it for their own partisan goals. I don't like that, but I understand it. The hostility of radical Islam to US interests is the defining national security challenge of our time, and the events in Benghazi are part of that story. All our team can do is share our perspective from the ground. We wanted to make sure the story of the events on the night of September 11, 2012, got told on our terms. Four Americans died that night: Chris Stevens, Sean Smith, Tyrone Woods, and Glen Doherty. Their deaths demand that we continue to set the record straight. I continued to do that after the publication of our book and the movie that Michael Bay directed based on our story. Talking about that night, and hearing the questions and comments from all the good people who have cared to listen, made me realize that some people are interested in understanding why we never quit and why we were all willing to act against our orders and risk the ultimate sacrifice in that situation. I began to reflect on the way our story unfolded, the reasons we were able to act as effectively as we did, and how my training and experiences might have contributed to my own performance at that critical moment.

SEPTEMBER 11, 2012

At 9:32, the consulate called the Annex for help because it was under attack. I know you might read elsewhere that the attack started at 9:42, but I looked at my watch when we got the radio call and feel clear about it having been 9:32. Our security team was at the Annex, which was about three-quarters of a mile to a mile away from the consulate, depending on how you traveled there.

When we got that call at 9:32 that night, saying "GRS, we need you in the team room now," I remember thinking "What did I do?" I wasn't the only one. My friend Dave "Boon" Benton asked me, "Tanto, what did you do now? Did you screw with someone today?" Sometimes I found the case officers pretentious and liked having a little fun at their expense. I had been deploying for ten years at that point, and I felt pretty free to mess around and joke with people. But I had been on good behavior, so I looked at Boon and meant it when I said, "I don't think I did anything."

Another call came on the radio about thirty seconds later, and it was intense. If you've been in the military or maybe in law enforcement, you know what I'm talking about when I say it was the kind of call that makes the hair on the back of your neck stand up. Not because you're scared, not exactly, but because it's exciting. You're about to get some action. So when we got the second call that said "GRS, we need you in the team room now!" Boon and I looked at each other again. We had been together for ten years at that point—in Iraq, Afghanistan, and Pakistan—and we could read each other's minds. He smiled at me, and I was thinking "Man, we're gonna do something fun tonight." We didn't realize, yet, that Americans were under attack.

We gathered our things and were headed toward the team room in Building C when the GRS team leader told us that the consulate was being overrun. We could hear gunfire and shouting in the distance. We were jocked up and ready to move five minutes after the initial call. We six contractors had all been in the Middle East for a few months before the attack, and we were a good team. Our Marines were Boon, a scout sniper with whom I had partnered before; Mark "Oz" Geist, a former police chief, and John "Tig" Tiegen, our two Navy SEALs were Jack Silva and Tyrone "Rone" Woods, and I was the only Ranger. Boon was my closest friend in Benghazi. I know it might sound odd to some of you military types to have a Ranger and a Marine be best friends, but it did happen. Jack and Rone had partnered together before as well. Tig had spent the most time in Libya. I had been there for about five months, part of that time in Tripoli. All of us had been deploying as either servicemen or contractors for at least ten years. We were an experienced team used to working in risky environments. If we are hired, it means the location is dangerous for case officers, so our postings are not in places like Jamaica or the Bahamas. But it is a rewarding job, and we had all continued to come back for more.

We were all in our late thirties or early forties, which is pretty old for combat. All of us had young children, too. Tig's wife had just had twins. Ty's wife just had baby Kai. I had a two-year-old. Jack had just found out that his wife was pregnant. All of us who wound up in this no-win, disadvantaged situation were new fathers. But not one of us would flinch. We might see things differently, but I believe it's because we had faith in one another, faith in God, and faith in the knowledge that we were all exactly where we were supposed to be.

Benghazi during the fall of 2012 was dangerous. Tripoli had been relatively safe, but Benghazi kind of felt like the

Wild West. It reminded me of being in Iraq in 2004 but without the military presence. There was no reliable police force, there was limited intelligence, and you never knew if you could trust what you were getting. Islamist militias were in charge of the city. But September 11 was an ordinary day, for Benghazi. The consulate was calm. We called it the consulate; I think the government called it a Special Mission. The distinction between a US Mission or Special Mission and a consulate is important because a Temporary Mission Facility or a Special Mission Unit requires less security than a consulate. The US government treated our location in Benghazi as a temporary residential facility, which didn't require it to officially notify the Libyan government of its existence and exempted it from the facility and accountability standards a consulate requires. State Department personnel have testified that the status of the US Mission in Benghazi was unlike anything in their working memory.

It was a relatively quiet night. Nothing out of the ordinary was happening. We conducted normal operations all day until about nine that night, and there were no reports of any videos or any insurrections. We would have been told of any kind of unusual activity. I think the locals knew the Annex was there. If they saw Americans coming out of there every day, including Ambassador Stevens, they might not have known the buildings belonged to the CIA, but they would have known it was part of the US government.

John and Rone had driven right in front of the consulate on patrol at 9:00 p.m. and called Dave Ubben, the diplomatic security agent there, to see if they should stop by. They were told, "No, we're good." Our role was to protect CIA staff, so we did not have a direct role with the consulate. We shared radios with the consulate and kept in regular contact, but keeping an eye on it was more of a handshake arrangement. It was out of our normal scope of duties to protect it. But we would have helped anyone who asked us. If you need help, call us; we'll come get you. We would have done that for any Americans. I think that is how we all understood our jobs as a Ranger, Marine, or SEAL. But we were contractors, and when you are a contractor, there are repercussions for not following orders or going beyond your scope of duties.

For example, people don't realize that contractors are not directly insured by the government. We are insured by a third party through Defense Base Act (DBA) insurance. If we had died or been injured at the consulate, working outside our normal scope of duties, we would not have been covered by that insurance. So we could have had no medical insurance after an injury, our families could have received no life insurance payout if we died. We could have been fired, or we could have lost our security clearance. Not one of us discussed it at the time, but we were all aware of the risks we could face, in addition to death. But Americans were in trouble. Americans needed help, and we wanted to take action. But we were told to wait.

Our team was ready to go within five minutes of the initial call, but it sounded as though we would be facing a substantial force, so the GRS team leader told us to wait while he

coordinated with a friendly local militia called 17 February
Martyrs Brigade (17 Feb). We were double- and triple-check-
ing our gear and waiting with our feet on the gas pedals of our
cars for ten or fifteen minutes. The compound was less than
a mile away; we could have walked there in the amount of
time we spent waiting. It was tough because we could hear the
State Department guys on the radio, and it was heartbreak-
ing. We could hear Scott Wickland, and we could hear Alec
Henderson, who was barricaded in the tactical operations
center, watching his team get decimated on video screens and
unable to do anything about it. He was saying "GRS, where
are you? GRS, where are you at? GRS, we need you. GRS,
we're taking heavy fire. GRS, you swore you'd get here." That
one really hurt. Because we had sworn to help. We'd given
our word.

I had approached our chief of base, Bob, and the team
leader and asked them to request air support and other
resources. They'd told me to hold up because 17 Feb might
be able to handle the whole thing themselves. I was incredulous. American lives were on the line, and we were letting
the initiative go while waiting to see if a foreign force (that
I didn't consider particularly reliable) might come to the rescue? We could still hear the firefight. I was trying to maintain my composure. I prayed, "God, just give me strength.
Give me strength to be patient. I want to burst out of this gate,
but I know I have to listen to my leaders." But sometimes a
moment comes when you have to stop listening to man's law
and start listening to God's law. That moment came for us at

about the fifteen-minute mark that night. I remember hearing
Scott and Alec on the radio and looking at Tig. Tig had gotten
out of his car and I could see him arguing with Bob. He was
telling him that we had to go, that we were losing the initiative. Bob said we could not go. Tig got back into his car, and
I asked "What's going on?" He told me, "Bob is saying we've
got to stand down."

That stand-down order has become a political hot but-
ton. Some people on the news claim it didn't happen. I don't
want to get into the politics around that, and I honestly feel it
doesn't matter anymore. I think the truth about Benghazi has
prevailed. If you want to take CNN's word over a Marine's,
go right ahead. Me, I'll take the Marine's word one hundred
percent of the time. We were told to stand down. And we continued to follow orders. That was what we had been trained
to do. But we had also been trained to fight and to protect
Americans at any cost. When we talked about it later, all the
guys agreed that we had each begun to think that soon we
might have to take the lead.

At about the twenty-five-minute mark, we heard Alec
Henderson say on the radio, "GRS, if you don't get here, we're
all gonna fuckin' die." Boon and I told our team leader, "We
need to go. Get in the fucking car." He did it. Rone cracked
the door of his car, and I could see his arm. If you've never
seen him on television, Rone was a big dude, SEAL Team 6.
All SEALs get big, but he looked like Leonidus, the warrior
king of Sparta. I remember seeing his huge arm, like a ham
hock, come out of this big door and motion to us. He made a

fist and flashed a thumbs-up. I thought, "I can't believe I get to be in this situation. I am going into combat with Leonidus." I gave him a thumbs-up in return and we started to move.

I was driving an SUV with Boon by my side and our GRS team leader in the back along with an interpreter from the Annex, Henry. Some interpreters are trained for combat, but Henry, who had always reminded me of an Egyptian Bob Newhart, was not one of them. His act of courage that night was amazing. I knew it would be useful to have a linguist to help us communicate with the 17 Feb force, so I had been trying to raise Henry on the radio while we were waiting. He was nowhere to be found, and I was feeling frustrated that we were going to waste more time while I ran around the Annex trying to find the guy. But it would be helpful to have him. God really was with us that night, because I got out of my car and Henry walked right in front of me. I said, "Henry, we need you."

He looked at me, and he knew I was about to ask him to go with us. He knew, and his eyes were huge behind his glasses. I said, "Look, Henry, I've been through this before, we need you. I need a local, somebody who speaks Arabic, because we don't speak it well enough and I don't want a friendly firing snit with a local force."

"Tanto," Henry protested, "I'm not weapons qualified."

"It doesn't matter," I told him. I handed him my pistol and said something like "You are now, go get your stuff."

Henry did not hesitate. "Roger that," he said, and my Bob Newhart grabbed the pistol and ran back into Building C, where all our gear was. He came back minutes later, dressed in body armor and a helmet that was way too big for him. As he ran toward our car looking like a turtle with a cockeyed shell, I felt amused and also full of pride and admiration for his guts. I don't want to put words in Henry's mouth, but I believe that Henry accepted that God had him where he needed to be. It might sound strange to describe a moment before battle as anything other than terrifying and grim, but the reality is that there can also be humor, there can be faith, and there can be love. And we were about to go do what we had trained to do: we were going to fight.

We drove our cars toward the compound and tried to plan. We had moved out without any clear plan regarding the 17 Feb militia. We were not sure how many of them were gathering, if any, or whether they knew we were coming. We decided to take a back route to the Annex to avoid any friendly fire and to try to minimize our chances of being seen by the enemy. As we got close to where we would normally make a right to go down near the consulate to the road we needed to be on, which was called Gunfighter, we realized we couldn't do it that way because we had started taking fire. The air echoed with snaps and cracks. The consulate compound had been set on fire by now, and we could see black smoke swirling out above our target. It took us about thirty minutes to fight our way about 400 meters to the consulate on foot. Boon and I, along with two friendly militiamen, climbed up several eight-foot walls and two buildings with the intention of getting a clear vantage point on the compound from the building on the other side. Jack, Tig, and Rone moved up to approach the compound from the main road. By the time we actually got to the consulate, more than an hour had passed from that first call, even though we were only about three-quarters of a mile away. We knew it was on fire and had seen the smoke and the orange glow in the sky as we approached it, but when I finally pulled up over that back wall, it was stunning. You might have seen some of the reports on the news: it was a massive blaze, with thick tornados of black smoke billowing up toward the sky. I remember looking at that fire rage, feeling its heat, and wondering if anyone in there could still be alive.

For the next hour, we fought bad guys over that nine-acre compound and tried to find survivors. We also found a dead body. That is always hard, always a serious obstacle. Boon came up to me shortly after 11:00 at the villa and said the words you don't ever want to hear in battle: "We lost one." He was pissed. Boon never gets angry, so when he does it scares me. He said, "If we just would have left on time, when we wanted to leave, he'd still be alive." I asked who we'd lost, and he said "the IT guy." For a minute I thought "Who is that?" and then immediately realized, "Ahhh, Sean." Sean had been there for only a few days. He had been counting on us. Boon was as pissed as I've ever seen him. But you can never quit, you can never stop fighting. I knew we still had a long night ahead of us, and I looked at him and just said, "Sergeant, relax!" and he snapped back into focus. Boon is a professional; he had been doing this for a long time. He said, "I'm good." I asked, "Are you sure?" and then he got pissed at me and said, "Dude, I'm good." I knew he was OK if he was getting mad at me.

I have been doing this work for ten years and I've got some scratches and scars, but I've never been shot or even caught shrapnel. I've been very blessed because it's not as though I haven't seen a few things. Sean had been there for just a few days, and now he was gone. At a moment like that, you have every reason to despair, to be reflective, to be pissed as hell. But you can't quit. At that point, you simply need to keep fighting. The ambassador was still missing, and we still didn't know if anyone was coming to help.

We were counterattacked at around 11:30, and we fought back with everything we had. We just shot and fought, and I was trying to be as aggressive as I could, hoping the enemy would be intimidated by our firepower and fall back. I initially took cover behind a car but felt I was wasting time. I flashed back to my Ranger instructors, some of whom had been part of Operation Just Cause in 1989. We had discussed their ops and I thought about how those Rangers had described shooting their way across an airfield in Panama right out in the open. I decided that shooting my way forward was my best chance to push the bad guys back. I remember taking a knee out in the open because there was no cover at all. I felt a physical sense of protection, almost as though there were a cocoon around me. It felt as though God had me. I remember hearing the sound of the snaps from the AK-47s bursting through the atmosphere. Sometimes you can hit the wrong spot and it's like stirring up a hornet's nest, but sometimes you hit the right spot and the fighting will stop. That is what finally happened. Then we received a report saying that bad guys were massing at the Annex and that the personnel there needed us to make our way back there and defend it. All of a sudden we were the most popular guys in town. We headed toward the Annex, which the enemy started to approach at approximately 12:30 p.m.

Part of the fifth stanza of the Ranger Creed, which I know by heart, is "I will never leave a fallen comrade to fall into the hands of the enemy." But we did. When we returned to the Annex, we left the ambassador behind. I will struggle with that call for the rest of my life. It violated my principles. Even if you are being left behind, you still don't leave someone else. Yet we left the ambassador. He was found at one in the morning in the back of the safe room. I can say that we were needed at the Annex. I can say that we could not get back far enough into the consulate because the fire was so strong and the smoke was so thick. But it doesn't matter, we left him. No excuses. It still haunts me. I try to trust that I can handle it because I believe that God never gives you more than you can handle.

The night was not done yet. We had three more firefights back at the Annex, and they were pretty vicious. We stationed ourselves on the rooftops of the buildings at the Annex and watched the attackers move toward us in waves through the misty fields we called Zombieland. All I was thinking up on that roof was how much I didn't want to let my buddies down. We were fighting for one another as much as anything else, and it was a beautiful thing. It's hard to see a relationship where people are protecting one another and fighting together in other places. I think it's one of the things that many former military guys like about contract work in the first place, the chance to still be part of a team of guys who will be there for one another.

Bub Doherty was a member of the Tripoli-based GRS team that chartered a plane from an oil executive to get the team from Tripoli to Benghazi to help us. We laughed about it later, teasing that they had flown to us in style on a G6 with fancy leather seats. But it's not funny that no US air assets helped us that night. Nobody. I am not in a position to understand who or how that decision was made. The official story is that the Department of Defense had no nearby armed drones or manned aircraft available for combat. But I believe, despite what anyone might testify, that air support was available. I don't know if the decision makers—whether they were at the State Department, the Department of Defense, the CIA, or the administration, I don't know—understood that the attack was going to be as bad as it turned out to be. But Bub and his team got there, and they got to our compound. They never quit and found a way.

Once they got to the Annex to help us evacuate, Bub was the only one of the group to climb up on to Building C and connect with Ty, Oz, and Dave Ubben, who were still in their fighting positions there. I remember hearing a sound like the swoosh of a rocket being launched. A mortar sounds more like a *fwomp*. My hearing was compromised after the long night of shooting, and it didn't sound like a mortar. When I served in Iraq, we had mortars fired at us all the time. It was so common that I would sometimes put in earplugs and go to sleep rather than running to a bomb shelter. So I know what mortar sounds like. It didn't sound like that. But that's what I thought it had to be.

I said, "Mortar, mortar, take cover," and as soon as I did, it hit. I started shooting. Everybody turned and started shooting because we were being attacked from the back side of Building C. There was no fear. We had been at it for eight and a half hours, but we weren't done yet because we don't give up. The enemy wasn't giving up either. I saw another mortar hit. When you see a mortar hit with your night vision goggles, your vision turns white for a few seconds before you can see again. I saw Dave go down. I could hear Dave say, "I'm hit!" Even with all that fighting and both your ears blown out, you can hear when a man thinks he is going to die. I can't replicate the terror in his voice. I looked behind me to make sure we were not being hit from the direction the mortars were coming from, and then I looked back again. More mortars hit, and my team just disappeared. It was as though they had evaporated. An explosive cloud blinded my night vision, and then all I could see was charged sparkling dust showering back down. In that moment, I thought, "We can't beat this." We still had no air support. But God kicked me in the back of the head and said, "Get your gun up, Ranger." I got my gun up, and I started shooting again.

We were asked over the radio to check in by fighting position. There was no response from Building C. Rone and Bub died in that blast. Dave Ubben's leg was sheared almost off, and he had serious wounds on his left arm below the elbow. Oz's body was pierced everywhere by shrapnel and his arm was almost blown off, but he was still trying to shoot with it. His arm would not cooperate and kept flopping down every time he tried to raise it. Oz eventually climbed down from that roof on his own with one arm. That is just toughness. He slipped once coming down on the bloody rungs of the ladder and caught himself with his bad arm. He never quit. He actually walked all the way into Building C, into our casualty collection center.

By the time we were able to evacuate everyone from the mission and the Annex to the airport, it was after 6 a.m. There was one airplane there, and it was the plane that Bub's team had chartered to get to us. It wasn't big enough for everyone, but Dave and Oz, who were both in bad shape, were among the passengers. That was how Bub saved lives that night. His never-quit attitude, his tenacity in renting that plane and figuring out how to get to us, saved Dave and Oz's lives because they were able to get back to Tripoli in time to receive critical medical attention. You never know what your outcome might be. You must keep pushing on.

I stayed behind, along with Jack, Boon, Tig, the two Delta Force operators, and the Tripoli-based GRS team who had arrived that morning. The bodies of Sean Smith, Rone, and

Bub would travel with us, and so would that of Ambassador Stevens, which had been recovered and brought to us that morning at the airport. At 10:30, we watched a hulking Libyan C130 touch down. I was relieved to be getting out of there, but I'm not going to lie: when I looked at that C130, a cargo plane with a Libyan flag on the tail, my heart sank a little. I had given eighteen years of my life to my country. I had been fighting all night for the United States, and we had lost guys. And a Libyan airplane was picking me up. The fact that we were flying out on another country's airplane after what had happened struck me as symbolic of the lack of US support we had had all night. I remember thinking "Still no Americans" and wondering, on the flight to Tripoli, how differently events might have unfolded if we had received the support we had asked for from the beginning. I remember thinking that Rone and Bub would still have been alive if we had gotten that support.

They flew us back to Tripoli, and we made our way from there to the Air Force base in Germany with not much more than our weapons and the clothes on our backs. God bless the USO: it fixed me up with new shoes and clothes, and I was able to take a moment to let the events of the last day sink in. We had lost Rone and Bub. Oz and Dave had gotten hurt. We had not saved the ambassador or Sean Smith. Yet it could have been much worse. By many calculations, it should have been much worse.

We were a skilled, experienced group but we had still been just six guys fighting through the night. But none of the guys on our team had a panic bone in his body, and we had made the most of every resource and opportunity that had presented itself. I believe part of our performance that night reflected the character, planning, discipline, endurance, and mental toughness that our military training as special operators demanded. For me, Benghazi was a test that called upon every resource and experience from my training and work as a Ranger. And I believe that many of the lessons learned on my journey to becoming a Ranger can be used by anyone who wants to pursue a goal that feels impossible.

Chapter Three

BE BRAVE

Energetically will I meet the enemies of my country . . . under no circumstances will I ever embarrass my country.
—RANGER CREED

You discover how brave you can be when someone or something you love is threatened. I love America. Some academics—I like to call them the smaht kids with my best Boston accent—try to make this complicated, but it is actually very simple: patriotism is loving, respecting, and serving your country. I am a patriot, and it makes me brave. The time I have spent overseas makes me feel grateful to be an American citizen, confident that the United States is the greatest country on earth, and determined to defend this country and our values. That does not mean I don't respect or admire some other countries. But I think the United States is special, and I'm not worried about offending the politically correct when I say that. The American flag means something to me when I see it raised, and I am willing to give my life to protect a fellow American if I have to. I think I've proved that.

I wear my beliefs and experiences on my body. I've got a lot of scars and a bunch of tattoos. One of my tattoos is a flag on the left side of my rib cage that gives the appearance that my skin is getting ripped open and there is an American flag inside of me. The flag is colored red and blue, and the stars are white. I have a Ranger scroll and Ranger tab on my left arm and a crusader cross on my left bicep, with the Ranger crest outlined on it. It symbolizes keeping my own demons in check and also symbolizes my job.

Rangers are like avenging angels and guardian angels, who are pushing back the evil in this world. There is evil out there, and certain people don't understand that. Many of us want to believe that everyone and everything can be reasoned with. The facts, to me, suggest otherwise. Sometimes you can't reason with other people. Sometimes they will kill you, either purposefully or because they just don't care if you happen to be in their line of evil fire. I think this is hard to see clearly when you are living in the United States.

I don't do what I do because of politics. Once the bullets start to fly, all the political bullshit goes out the window. Bullets do not care about your party affiliation, race, gender, or anything else. Once an operation starts, I am focused on my job and my job has been part of a larger interest, like protecting the country; helping to stop terrorism; or helping destroy or disrupt an attack. Make no mistake, the United States will continue to see lone-wolf attacks against us. Political correctness and partisan differences must be set aside to fight them.

We must protect ourselves, and you can't be afraid to say what you really mean.

* * *

I was born in Alamosa, Colorado, a small town on the Sangre de Cristo mountain range, where I spent the early part of my childhood. My mother was my first-grade teacher, and my father was a football coach at Adams State College. I have a younger brother and older sister, and the elementary school we went to was way out in the middle of nowhere.

My brother and I are only a year and a half apart, so we played together constantly growing up. We spent most of our time outside, climbing trees, riding bikes, looking for little bird's nests and going toad hunting. At that time and place, parents weren't too worried about their kids playing around the neighborhood, so my golden lab and I would routinely roam on our own to the river about a mile away from our house. No one thought anything of it.

I loved to fish with my grandfather, and I was always out shooting and hunting jackrabbits. I think I got my first BB gun in first or second grade. All the neighbor kids used to have BB gun fights, but our parents stopped that when I shot my brother by accident. My mom gave me a good whipping with my gun and broke it, but my dad felt sorry for me and eventually got me another one. By the time I was in third grade, I had a motorbike and I got in a few good wrecks with that and hurt myself some, but it didn't seem like a big deal.

All that activity and independence seemed very normal, and I think it has served me well.

The childhood I'm describing might sound pretty western and traditional, but my family has our immigrant heritage, which is also part of the American story. My full given name is Kristian Joaquin Paronto. The Joaquin is for my grandfather on my mother's side, Joaquin Garcia. He was an immigrant from Mexico with an incredible work ethic who came to this country with nothing and eventually built up his own farm in Delta, Colorado. I spent a lot of my childhood running around that land, picking asparagus or shooting, hunting, or fishing. My grandmother's heritage was Mexican and Navajo Indian. My Spanish is just OK, but it comes rushing back when I'm immersed in a primarily Spanish-speaking environment.

My family fit in with the Mexican community, which was prevalent in Alamosa, where I lived, and in Delta, where my grandparents lived at that time. My brother and I spent time with the kids and migrant workers whose families worked the nearby farms, playing baseball, football, and having rock fights on the country roads. One of the migrant workers from Mexico might have even saved my life when I was around seven years old. We were playing hide-and-seek, and I cracked my head open on the back of a potato truck. I was bleeding, but I had been hiding, so nobody knew where I was. My cousin stumbled over me and ran for help, and it was one of the migrant workers helping on my grandparents' farm who carried me back to my grandma in his arms.

I grew up believing that the United States is the greatest country in the world, but I did not grow up wanting to be an Army Ranger. I started to think about serving, generally, when I was a student at Mesa State University and began to talk with recruiters from different branches of the military. The Army recruiter in the student center showed me a video from the 75th Ranger Regiment, and I was intrigued. I remember asking him, "Do guys ever quit when they're trying to become Rangers?" He replied with an emphatic, "YES!!" and I was sold. I wanted to test myself. It seemed tough, but I don't think I really understood what I was joining until I actually got into the Army. Seeing men who had been serving as Rangers for their whole careers was inspiring. The respect that other guys in the military showed me when I said I was planning to be a Ranger was motivating. Once I actually began training and testing to be a Ranger, I knew I had found my path.

Army Rangers, Navy SEALs, Delta Force operators, Green Berets, Air Force Pararescuemen, MARSOC (US Marine Corps Forces Special Operations Command), and other elite forces in various military branches are part of the special operations community. The different branches of the military have unique areas of expertise and some distinctive forms of training, but all special ops units are made up of skilled soldiers, Rangers, Marines, seamen, and airmen who have trained and tested in special selection courses under intense and brutal conditions. The 75th Ranger Regiment is the largest special ops combat element in the US Army and the best light infantry fighting force on the planet. Rangers can be sent to the front lines and beyond, deep into enemy territory. If special ops forces are called in, it's going to be a high-pressure situation. We are expected to perform not just adequately but heroically, no matter what is going on. We are trained to be a strike force that can be called on to rescue civilians, prisoners of war, or other forces in trouble; to go into hostile territory to monitor or assess enemy operations; and to seize, destroy, or capture enemy airfields and facilities.

* * *

Our team in Benghazi were all former special operators and Marines who brought our training, skills, and commitment to bear on September 11, 2012. We had all been prepared for operations that might be riskier than regular military operations either because of different techniques being used or because there could be fewer assets and less support than there might be in a conventional battle.

What makes someone volunteer to put his life on the line by going into enemy territory? For me, it is patriotism, love, and gratitude for the blessing of my citizenship. I grew up believing that the United States was the greatest, most powerful nation in the world. I took many of the comforts and freedoms we enjoy for granted. Many Americans still take the rights and freedoms established in the Constitution for granted. Some want to pick and choose among constitutional rights and downplay some of them, such as the right to bear arms, to worship as we will, or to speak freely. I believe the threats against our freedoms are real. We need to name those threats and fight them when we see them, with honesty and integrity.

*   *   *

Whenever I come home to the United States after working overseas, it is like taking a trip to Disneyland. Americans do not appreciate how well we have it. Now, you might find it hard to feel the truth of that if you are struggling to get by. Or you might be skeptical because you have just returned from a vacation overseas and things looked pretty good wherever you were staying. No. People all around the world are suffering in ways most of us in the United States don't have to think about. Children are hungry and unsafe, living in chaotic and hopeless situations. I don't recommend it, but go live in one of the places I've been and immerse yourself in the culture, eat the food, and live off the local economy, and then get back to me. Many Americans do not appreciate the simple reality that we are largely able to go about our daily lives and pursue our goals freely and safely, without the threat of government repercussions and without the real possibility of an IED explosion while we're out running our errands. Maybe some of us have a little more of that fear now, but it cannot be compared to the situations in which many people live around the world.

My views are informed by my time on the ground and the many episodes of violence I have witnessed. A particular day in Baghdad in 2005 while I was providing security for the State Department is never far from my mind. I was the detail leader for a visit that the acting ambassador was making to the compound of a local imam in the Mansour district of Baghdad. This was not a covert operation. We were the visible security for the Department of State, and I was there with a huge team all day. The meeting between the ambassador and the imam lasted for several hours, and I was working outside the compound all day. The atmosphere was tense, and the visit was attracting a lot of local attention. My buddy Joe noticed civilians using their cell phones to take pictures of our armored Suburbans and the Humvees of the military convoy that had come with us. A black Mercedes sped up and seemed to be starting to make a run at the front gate of the compound, but Joe went out with a mini–machine gun and drew down on the car from about seventy-five feet away. He deterred the car, which went flying past the compound. So a few things felt eerie, but, at the same time, it was a pretty normal day in Baghdad.

People were going about their normal activities in the neighborhood, and children were playing at their homes. I remember seeing two schoolgirls play in the yard across the street from the back gate of the imam's compound. They looked like sisters, maybe seven or eight years old, in little jeans and T-shirts and plastic flip-flops. They were bouncing a ball and playing outdoors in their yard all day. I'm careful when I interact with local children overseas because I don't ever want to frighten them or get them into trouble, but I also want to be friendly and have them think well of us. At some point during the day, I waved at them, and one of them waved shyly and smiled and then kept playing. I thought about how surreal it must have been to have our kind of security detail as the background of their normal childhood activity.

When it was time for the ambassador to leave, I went ahead with a military Humvee to set up a tactical control point (TCP) about a quarter of a mile away for his trip back to the embassy. When you set up a TCP, you block an intersection so that the person you are protecting can go through quickly and avoid an attack. When you are stopped at an intersection, you can become a vulnerable target for a vehicle bomb, especially if you seem as if you might be of high value. We set up and waited for the ambassador, who was taking longer than expected. As you can imagine, any delays were annoying to the locals because we were tying up their traffic. As we waited and traffic backed up, another US military convoy going about its own business in the other direction got stuck in the roadblock, too. Finally, the ambassador's car shot through, and I guided the convoy to bypass the line while we held the TCP for the trail team that was following the ambassador. As I waited, feeling good that we were about to wrap up the day up, there was a huge explosion. A VBIED (vehicle-borne improvised explosive device) had detonated at the imam's compound. Even from my distance, I could feel it rattle the ground and see the smoke and dust that immediately rose into the sky, carrying debris. I called the trail team on the radio, confirmed that they were OK, and held the TCP for them to get through. Our whole team was, miraculously, intact. As we followed them back toward the embassy into the Green Zone, I saw one of the helicopters we called Little Birds peel off back toward the explosion site.

When the pilot returned, he was upset and full of news about our close call. It sounded as though a black Mercedes had set up by the back gate of the compound and the other military convoy that I had let through the TCP had gotten hit. I don't know if it was the same car that had taken a run at the front gate earlier in the day. And I don't know if the convoy just became a target of opportunity as it drove by, but it was hit and a soldier in an upper turret of the Humvee was injured. The Little Bird picked him up, and the pilot told me about flying him back for medical help. He also told me about seeing a father holding his little girl, who had been cut in half by that VBIED. I felt sick because I knew he was talking about one of the girls I had watched playing off and on all day long. The girls had been in their own yard, right across from the back gate.

* * *

About a month before the VBIED exploded in front of those little girls, I was standing on Haifa Street in Baghdad, right outside a spot known as Little Assassins' Gate when a big cargo truck came flying toward me. I raised my machine gun in one hand, pinched all five fingers of my other hand together, and raised them skyward. That is called "the onion," and people understand it to mean "back off." The truck kept coming. I had seconds to make a decision about whether to pull my trigger. I considered the truck, thinking that normally a VBIED would be smaller. There appeared to be more than one person in the cab of the truck, which was also not normal for a car bomb. As they got closer, I could see that one of the passengers was a kid. The car screeched to a stop about fifteen feet in front of me. The man driving looked terrified, and so did the young boy, about seven or eight years old, sitting next to him. I approached the cab slowly with my gun up and pulled a picture of my own son out of my pocket. I put it up against the window so they could see it. I pointed back and forth between the picture and myself, and then I pointed at his son and smiled. The driver relaxed, smiled, and pulled over.

GRS guys are often assigned to protect diplomats, but I sometimes think that we were ambassadors in our own way. Official ambassadors spend their time meeting with ministers and dignitaries. We are interacting with people on the ground, and in some cases we are the first Americans they meet. That is why it is critical that GRS operators not be tightly wired all the time.

* * *

The reality of my job is that we aren't sent anywhere to make friends. We are trained to protect and defend, which sometimes requires attacking. Ranger training is all about preparing for the reality of what that means. Before you can go to Ranger School, first you must go through what is now called the Ranger Assessment and Selection Program (RASP). When I was going through training it was called the Ranger Indoctrination Program (RIP), and that is how I am going to refer to it here. The experience is always changing, but the purpose of the program is to teach the basic skills required of a Ranger and to assess a soldier's ability to be a member of the 75th Ranger Regiment. I entered it after I completed basic training and Airborne School.

On the first full day of RIP, everyone was medically processed and we were assigned to our rack at the barracks, four guys to a room. There were paintings and murals on the old cinder-block walls of the hallways in our barracks. There were images of scrolls with Ranger berets and one of a Ranger shooting an M-16. I don't know who painted them or when they were painted. They felt a little like accomplished graffiti or even a public art project, not unlike what you'd see in a park, except for the subject matter. I walked to the end of a long hallway to get my linens and stopped in my tracks. There was a life-sized painting of a Viet Cong from the torso up, and his head was exploding with a bullet through it. It was large, technically skillful, realistic, and shocking. It felt authentic, as though the artist had known what he was painting. I was reminded, when I looked at it, that war is death. Of course, I had thought about that many times, but there was something about seeing that painted image in that space that was different from watching a movie. These guys are death dealers, I thought, and I'm training to join them. I remember wondering if I was doing the right thing. Am I OK to kill somebody like that? Right in the head? I wasn't sure how to interpret the image, either. Was it promoting death? Almost celebrating it? I couldn't decide. I wondered if this was right and whether I should quit.

If anyone quit over that picture, I'll never know. But it gave me a good rattling, and I imagine it rattled some other guys too. It is important to acknowledge the reality of war. War is not reasonable. War happens when you can no longer reason with the enemy. People will die. They will die in awful ways. It's important to acknowledge the gravity of what you could be asked to do. I accepted it. This was going to be my job. I wasn't thinking "This is cool." You don't want to kill anybody, you want to live and let live in peace. But sometimes you have to kill people to keep other people safe and you have to kill people if they're trying to kill you. The enemy should know that if they push us, if they come after us, we will blow their heads right off.

* * *

Radical Islam is a threat to the United States. It is the defining national security challenge of our time. We will lose the battle if we don't get serious and coordinated about fighting it. I don't want us to experience in the United States what I got used to over the last ten years overseas, listening to gunfire and explosions and seeing people, including children, blown up in front of my eyes. It might be hard to wrap your head around it, but that could happen here if we don't stand up and fight.

People and policy makers need to listen to the men and women who have been immersed in that culture and who have actually fought on the ground. When I, or other veterans, speak about this, it is not based on things we have watched on television or read on Twitter. I believe that we need a series of congressional hearings and a new 9/11 Commission–style report to help us strategize properly. And I believe that the leadership of that commission should include elected representatives who actually have experience, on the ground, fighting in the Global War on Terror. People who watch the fight on monitors in a war room are not enough.

Pro-American Muslims have an important role to play in this battle. Particularly in Afghanistan, I have worked closely on the ground with many fine Muslim people who were working as interpreters or guarding our gates, and I was moved by their commitment to the United States.

In Kabul, our government was working with the Afghan National Army (ANA) to provide security for the outer perimeter of Camp Phoenix off of Jalalabad Road (we used to call it J-bad). The ANA's responsibilities included checking the identification of anyone who approached the main gate of the outer perimeter of the camp. Remote detonation of bombs was less frequent at that time, so if someone pulled up in a VBIED, he wanted to get as close as possible to the target before detonating himself by putting two wires together to initiate the explosion. The US military was the next gate down, so our forces were capable of quickly swarming a car or overpowering an enemy. The ANA was the first line of defense.

We started calling one of the guards on that team "Rambo." It was an unlikely nickname for an unassuming guy in his thirties who was about five feet seven, but he had guts. As cars approached the gate, the drivers had to roll down their windows to answer his questions or he wouldn't let them through. On at least three verified occasions, Rambo physically dived into a VBEID and fought to hold the driver's hands apart so that he could not detonate. Not once, not twice, but three times, this Afghan citizen stopped attacks on our military with his bare hands, by jumping in and putting his own body on the line to keep a terrorist from igniting a bomb.

Rambo was a man of extraordinary courage, as are many of the pro-American Muslims who take risks to help us overseas. There are many people of Middle Eastern heritage who love and admire America, who have served in and alongside US forces, and who have demonstrated real dedication to freedom. These people have enormous value in the fight against radical Islam. They are patriots and deserve our support. But we must also abandon political correctness and overhaul our vetting system for immigrants and refugees for every person coming in from anywhere, not only the Middle East.

WISDOM FROM THE RANGERS
PRINCIPLE ONE:
STAND UP AND BE BRAVE

When you have clarity about your values, you should be willing to defend them, and it then becomes easier to be brave. The men and women of our armed services risk their lives every day to protect you and your freedoms and opportunities. Most people don't need to literally put their lives on the line, but you might need to put yourself into the line of fire, metaphorically speaking, in order to stand up for what's right. Once you identify the values that are priorities for you, you need to be willing to sacrifice your time and energy in service to the goals that follow from them. If you are willing to be criticized or to sacrifice your peace of mind, your time, your safety, and possibly other tangible benefits in order to stand up for your values, that is acting with integrity and it is a valuable kind of courage. That's when you will find out how brave you can be.

Chapter Four

DEFINE YOUR MISSION

Know . . . Yourself, and the strengths and weaknesses in your character, knowledge, and skills. Seek continual self-improvement, that is, develop your strengths and work to overcome your weaknesses.
—*RANGER HANDBOOK,* "LEADERSHIP," 1–1

I feel as though I've had the best job in the world. It has been a blessing to have spent a good part of my professional life protecting and defending the United States, and I am proud to have served as an Army Ranger. The training to become a soldier, and then a Ranger, for the United States is as tough as, or tougher than, anything you've read about or seen in movies. Sometimes it was a struggle, and I'm going to tell you in these pages about many moments when I was humbled. But I really took to the training and felt I had found my purpose, even when it was very challenging. As a Ranger, my mission might have been to participate in a raid. As a member of the Global Response Staff, my mission might have been to secure an area or conduct an operation to protect people who were gathering information. But when I signed up, my mission was to become a member of the 75th Ranger Regiment and to protect the United States. That was a mission I understood, one I believed in, one that was aligned with my values and my personality. That's what carried me through the tough parts. You need to find your mission and set some goals.

If you have a worthy goal, by which I mean a goal you are going to need to work for, as opposed to a task you need to cross off your to-do list, it probably isn't going to be easy to achieve. If you intend to stick with it when the going gets tough, it's important to choose a mission that matters to you, one that you really believe in. In order to do that, you need to do some thinking about your own values and purpose. Think about who and what inspire you and what you really want. How badly do you want it? A good goal helps you get tough. The more you want it, the stronger the commitment you'll be able to make and the longer and harder you'll be willing to work and sacrifice for it.

* * *

My mission was to be a Ranger. Out of the three hundred people who graduated from Airborne School with me, fewer than fifty of us tried out for the 75th Ranger Regiment. Immediately after our graduation ceremony for Airborne School, we were told to stand in formation and wait. No one spoke. We stood at attention. It was August in Georgia, and I remember that the tension in the air felt as real as the heat. We could see our classmates falling out and joining their loved ones to celebrate earning their parachutist badges while we waited with all our possessions packed in duffel bags at our feet. Finally, big flat-bed trucks carrying guys in black berets and their starched and spits showed up. That was the Ranger Cadre from the 75th Ranger Regiment. They had a glassy spit shine on their boots and looked badass. We had heard all the rumors about the Ranger Indoctrination Program, and we knew they were the guys who were going to put us through hell for the next three weeks.

Drill sergeants in basic training get in your face and yell. We were used to that. The Ranger instructors were more intimidating. There was no screaming, but they would get right up in a guy's face and ask, "You want to be a Ranger, huh?" or "What the fuck are you doing here? You think you got what it takes?" The only acceptable answer was to say "Yes, Sergeant." We were a spectacle. People stopped to watch us get belittled, and I was surprised that the sergeants would curse in front of the civilians still milling around from the ceremony. It made them seem even more badass. They asked if anyone wanted to quit, and I was even more surprised when a couple guys raised their hands right there.

They brought over two big flatbed trucks. They told us we had thirty seconds to get all our gear loaded into the first one in the front. My heart was already racing, sweat was rolling down my back, and we hadn't even moved yet. We still all had that basic training mentality, so we ran and got it neatly stacked and done in about thirty seconds. The instructors seemed a little shocked, to be honest. But then they said,

"Wait, you idiots, we didn't tell you to load the first truck in the front, we said to put the bags in the second truck! Pay better attention! Do it in twenty seconds this time!" Nobody balked, and we did the transfer in twenty seconds. Well, maybe it was forty seconds, I can't remember. But I know it was quicker than shit and we got it done. Then they smoked us anyway, which meant doing push-ups, flutter kicks, and mountain climbers on the hot pavement. Those are all standard-issue military punishments. It did not matter that my RIP class had performed exceptionally well, loading and unloading those trucks in double time. We were doing calisthenics in the Georgia heat wearing our heavy-ass combat boots and winter BDUs because we didn't rate the summer ones yet. Most of us just stuck with it, but three more guys quit right there. They were not berated. There was no yelling "You don't even know what Army Ranger Battalion is about!"

The RIP cadre would nod, and maybe say, "Just go. Get out of line. Go somewhere else." And they went. I watched the RIP cadres and wondered if they really wanted us to quit. I was trying to control my stress. I was also realizing that there was a real opportunity for an out. That is important, because when you pass up an opportunity to quit, it builds your commitment and mental strength.

The RIP cadres were only just starting to mess with us. I came to think of things like the flatbed fiasco, where they try to trip you up, as fuck-fuck games. You will never win a fuck-fuck game, you will only endure it. Can you recite the Ranger Creed out loud, from memory, with no mistakes? Oh, and in twenty seconds? You can't. You are destined to fail at that task. As we did. But we tried to do it, looked like fools in front of strangers and one another, and then were berated when we failed. Why would your leaders ask you to do this? I believe that they wanted us to understand that some things are impossible but you've got to try anyway. You never quit. Are fuck-fuck games professional? No. But combat is not professional. It is dirty. It is unfair. And so is a lot of life. You need to work hard and try anyway, even when the odds are against you. That applies to everything in life, not just combat. I don't look back on the fuck-fuck games with any anger or resentment. They reinforced the idea that you do not give up, even when you seem all but set up for failure.

* * *

Ranger candidates are volunteers. In fact, the 75th Ranger Regiment uses *Sua sponte*, which means "Of their own accord" as its motto because you have to volunteer three times: once for basic training, once for Airborne School, and once for Ranger School. RIP is just the beginning of your third phase of volunteering, and it is something of a tryout. You are learning skills, but it's not like basic training or Airborne School, both of which I had already completed. The military needs people to graduate from basic and Airborne. Sure, people are dropped from those schools, but they are usually either injured or psychologically unfit for that particular kind of service. Airborne School is relatively easy; people don't usually quit. In basic training, you're going to be miserable for sixteen weeks and it's a good way to learn how to suck things up, but they aren't really trying to get you to quit. Basic training and Airborne School are both challenging and have painful moments, but RIP is made up of painful moments on steroids. Ranger Battalion does not need to pass people.

Ranger training focuses on teaching you how to perform in a state of deprivation and stress. That training is what you can look forward to after you pass RIP and if you distinguish yourself while serving as a private in the battalion. Why is the training so punishing? The idea is that if soldiers are operating in hostile territory, food, sleep, and support may be limited or nonexistent, so you need to train in those conditions. The Army wants to have confidence that you will be knowledgeable, remain focused, and be able to execute your goals under the most dangerous conditions possible.

The journey from basic training to elite training to deployment or combat is not simply challenging; many aspects of it just plain suck. Overcoming and embracing that suck changes a lot of things about a person, especially his or her mind-set. Military training requires self-discipline, resilience, and the willingness to look honestly at yourself and be humble if you want to improve your skills. We had to become faster and stronger; learn how to march, move, and shoot in full gear under pressure for time and accuracy; become competent in navigation and orienteering; get used to working during the day and night, in all kinds of weather conditions; confront obstacles designed to expose us to specific issues we might face in the field, such as developing the stamina to keep running or marching for an unknown amount of time, to jump from up high, or to crawl through an enclosed space; to plan and execute missions while everyone is in a state of physical and mental exhaustion; and to learn to do those things and function as a team when all are being pushed to their limits. Everyone tries and fails and succeeds, in front of one another, task by task, and you become brothers as well as soldiers.

Military training teaches you how to accomplish large missions by breaking them down into smaller goals. When soldiers learn infantry tactics in basic training, they do it in stages. Let's say we are assigned a training mission, such as clearing a bunker. Individual movement tactics are where we start: we have to learn how to move alone before we start moving and working as a team. So we drill and learn how to cover one another as we move down a field, in alternate and successive bounding, both alone and as part of a two-man team. We learn how to watch and move so that we don't shoot each other and so that we're covering the next team as they are coming down. We did not use live weapons during those early exercises; we were all learning how not to shoot our buddies! We used an older laser system called multiple integrated laser engagement system (MILES) gear, which required us to wear special harnesses that actually increased the suck factor because they were cumbersome and we had to clear out and set the lasers as we went, but they gave us feedback without injury. We learned how to function as guys went down, because we still had to continue without their assistance. Eventually we could move down a big field as a coordinated team. When we got to the actual bunker, that was the most challenging part of the drill. We were moving, shooting, and learning how to work together to take out an enemy, so that one team was sweeping around while another team created suppressive fire.

We went from doing exercises in a two-man team, to doing movements in a fire team of four. Then two teams learned to move together to do a squad attack. When we got competent at that, the platoon provided an opposing force. We were still not learning to do anything in a group bigger than a squad-sized element. Accomplishing those tasks successfully created goals and subgoals within our larger mission to become a soldier.

Our goals, or subgoals, need to be realistic and achievable. In military training, the tasks set for us build on one another, so the goals are realistic. For example, back in basic training, everyone learned about the standard ammo and weapons of an infantryman and could not graduate without qualifying on the M16, but they didn't throw us out on the range to qualify as a sharpshooter the first time we picked up an M16. No! It was broken down into stages.

First they gave us a weapon to disassemble and put back together. Then we spent time learning our trigger squeeze along with how to get a good site picture. We learned how to dry fire a weapon and stay steady. One type of exercise used to improve those skills was called dime-washer drills. We worked in teams: one guy aimed an M16 and the other guy inserted a cleaning rod into the barrel of the rifle so it stuck out about three inches and then balanced a dime or a little washer on top of it. The shooter needed to keep the dime from falling off. We took turns doing that, which was how we learned to stay steady. It's pretty tricky the first time you do it. As you get better, you practice keeping the dime on while you pull your trigger release back. Maybe after a week or so, you move from handling the weapon to aiming and shooting it. Now you are understanding proper site picture. Then you finally get out onto the range and shoot.

We had to get very accurate with our shooting in order to qualify: we would practice hitting targets from 50 to 300 meters out, and if we missed too many, we had to try again. Most people pass eventually, because during their down time the drill sergeants provide additional hands-on training for people who need it. But the requirements are broken down into many different subgoals on the way to the goal of qualifying as a sharpshooter. Qualifying on this test is itself a subgoal on the way to completing basic. We took it task by task and built our way toward the goal.

* * *

Here's the thing: we're not any better than you. I know I'm not. I'm an average guy who figured out what I wanted to do, learned how to get the skills and support I needed to reach my goals, and took charge of my life. In some ways, I'm still doing it because defining and executing one's life mission is an ongoing process. And believe me, mine has been a process of trial and error. The trials and errors can be dramatic because being a soldier involves confronting life-or-death situations. But most soldiers enter basic training as average guys, just like me, and we all face personal and professional challenges.

Most guys who walk into RIP on day one are in knots, nervous as hell, wondering if they are going to belong. Most special ops soldiers are in good physical condition, but they are not born with extraordinary abilities. They are not the absolute best at anything. They are regular guys who are willing to put their lives on the line and willing to sign up to be trained and challenged with that possibility in mind. I always think of the Bible passage "As a man thinketh, so is he." Everything that happens to us in the military improves on the average mind-set and instills courage, confidence, self-discipline, focus, patriotism, loyalty, obedience, and brotherhood.

There is a reason the United States has the greatest military in the world. Training needs to be tough because you want to be able to have your soldiers stay focused on completing their mission and field any circumstance they may encounter in a combat situation. I'm not here to tell you that you need to enlist in order to improve yourself, only that you can apply some of the tools of our training to reach your own goals. Rangers need discipline, focus, and endurance, and those are great skills for us all to have in the real world.

Confidence comes from competence. You won't understand the limits of your competence until you have tested them. If you are like most people, the limits of your competence are infinitely greater than you can imagine. They will be infinitely greater than you know if you refuse to settle and continue to set new goals for yourself. The guys who sign up for RIP have already met the goal of becoming infantrymen and becoming airborne qualified. RIP stretches the boundaries of their competence to their limits.

* * *

It was about a mile and a half to the base from Airborne School, and I had heard that normally we would all run there, following behind our stuff in the trucks. I don't know if it was the heat that day or our strong performance or what, but they let us ride in the back of that first truck like cattle with our gear following us in the second truck. I remember pulling up the road and laying eyes on the 75th Ranger Regiment for the first time. RIP is held at a different facility now, but we were approaching the old barracks, driving past a nine-foot-high chain-link fence that was woven through so you couldn't see in or out. I wondered if that was what it felt like to be a prisoner entering a maximum-security correctional facility for the first time. As we drove in, we could see a huge black asphalt basketball court with a big painting of a skull and beret with a scroll and tab at the half-court mark. That scroll was for the 75th Unit, and we were here to earn the tab and the beret. You could hear the slam as they shut the gate behind us after we drove through, and my heart felt heavy, as if I was being locked into a lion's den. But I thought, "Bring it on."

As soon as the truck stopped, it was game on for about two hours. We moved our fifty-pound bags back and forth, stacking and unstacking them for no discernible reason. We ran up and down the basketball court and did push-ups, sit-ups, and flutter kicks in that Georgia heat. I had to hold a plank with my back straight after the push-ups, and my hands were on fire because the sun had been baking the asphalt all day long. Day one at RIP is all about who really wants to be there. They were weeding us out, and we started to see what we could endure.

I try to think of a happy place when I'm going through something like that, maybe a big hill with tall grass blowing in the wind against a blue sky. Everyone's visualization is different; you can think about an island paradise, your childhood swimming hole, the image doesn't matter as long as it calms you down and gives you a focal point that distracts from the pain. I also remind myself that whatever crappy thing is happening is always going to end, one way or another.

It might sound counterintuitive, but I am motivated when other people collapse or quit. I don't mean that I'm rooting for anyone to fail, it's more that when I see someone quit, I might tell myself, "I'm stronger than him" or "I lasted longer than that" and it gives me a little fuel. We had a strong class, so I didn't have a lot of opportunity to get motivation that way the first day, but there was a steady stream of quitting as the week went on.

The day is never done at RIP, and I was constantly trying to keep up. But as I faced each challenge, I drew strength from the challenges I had already met and the guys who were shoulder to shoulder with me. What I might be facing was tough, but each day I drew confidence from the tough stuff I had already completed. And, boy, did they put us through some tough stuff. The physical training that started each morning at RIP was ungodly. Two-mile runs that had to be done in thirteen minutes or less. Five-mile runs in formation that had to be done in forty minutes. Twelve-mile forced ruck marches carrying a fifty-pound rucksack that had to be done in three hours. About fifteen guys quit during those runs.

The RIP cadre told us to be ready for PT at 5:00 a.m. on our first full day. There were some guys in our class who had recycled, which means they hadn't passed RIP the first time but had done well enough that they were invited to try again, so they knew what was coming. Those guys told us that the cadre might wake us up by coming down the hallways banging trash barrels and screaming and yelling. I hate being woken up like that, and I don't know who wouldn't. I don't think I slept at all that first night. I finally got up and showered around 4:00 a.m., trying to be quiet so the leaders couldn't see me. Actually, hiding is out of the question because there is no privacy in that environment. Imagine a large airport bathroom with no doors on the stalls, sinks lined up next to one another, and a big open shower in the back corner with multiple shower heads so eight guys can shower at a time. There is exactly zero time to be embarrassed to use the toilet or take a shower in public, you just have to get over it. There is some justification for it, because you do have to get used to living with guys in close quarters and worse situations. But I had managed to get that moment alone and I felt like a pilot on a runway, waiting for my signal to take off. Sure enough, I heard guys pounding up the stairs into the barracks, throwing metal trash cans down on the floor. "Get up, you've got five minutes to get outside!" and people went scrambling.

I thought, "OK, it's on, here we go." We went outside and started running. Rangers from the 75th Battalion are like gazelles: they must run, and they can't be slow. These are not formation runs, precisely, so you don't need identical cadence, but you have to keep up. The RIP sergeants are in excellent shape: they work out constantly and rigorously, running and marching with their guys. We ran to a PT field for physical fitness tests. I was in good shape, and I maxed the push-up and sit-up tests and passed but did not max my run, which was the first time I hadn't done so since my first run in basic training. I guess I had gone a little soft in Airborne School. Not maxing was disappointing for me, and I swore privately that I was going to get back into top form. When everyone finished and we were back in formation, there were some empty spots where a few guys had dropped out. It wasn't a public quitting. Every day, it seemed, I would look around and see a few empty spots and think, "Hey, where's Johnson?" or "Where's Smith?" and they just weren't there. They had quietly gone into the office to give notice, and I didn't know they were doing it. I felt a little sense of accomplishment about it, like "Well, I'm still here, that's good."

Sometimes the institutional response to a lot of people failing or dropping out of something is "Oh, crap, a lot of people are dropping, we have to lower the standards so that more people can make it." That's bullshit. Those difficult standards may be saving lives when they are on the line. We do not need to accept mediocrity. It's OK to excel. It's OK for different people to be better at different things. It's OK for people to realize what their strengths and weakness are and find the appropriate space for themselves. So push yourself to be your best and figure out if your best in some places is stronger or better than others. It usually is. But don't fudge the standards.

I found some of the running paces we were asked to keep seriously challenging, even though running is one of my physical strengths. Guys who were not great runners often felt as though we were being held to impossible standards. But you can't say, "I can't do this." You might as well go sit on your butt and suck your thumb. Work your tail off. Work as a team. You might fail, but see how far you can get when you tell yourself, "I can do this, I can do this, I can do this." That was the attitude we had in Benghazi on September 11, 2012: we were six guys against who knew how many people, and no one quit.

We didn't have many advantages that night. But we sure had clarity about our purpose. Being clear about your mission is your first advantage as you launch your campaign. The mission has to be genuinely important to you; if you believe in it, you will stay motivated. Also, don't be afraid to want to win.

Sometimes that's an advantage to having a mission in the military: you are crystal clear about wanting to win because people may die if you lose. So you do not accept failure because you know what it could mean. You need to want to win your civilian life battles with the same tenacity.

WISDOM FROM THE RANGERS

PRINCIPLE TWO: YOUR MISSION SHOULD REFLECT YOUR VALUES

You've got to start somewhere. I don't care where you're starting from or what kind of mistakes you made in the past. You may have made choices in the past that you regret. Think of them as bullets that are downrange now; you already shot them. You can't take those back, you can only adjust your aim for the next ones, so it's time to focus on your next move. You need to set some goals and launch a new campaign. Being clear about your mission will be your first advantage.

Everyone has personal battles. I don't know what yours are. You may be facing work conflicts, financial challenges, or problems in one or more of your relationships, with your family, your partner, your parents, or your children. Maybe you're dealing with a health issue such as alcoholism, drug dependency, obesity, or depression. Or maybe things are generally OK but you need a battle strategy to take yourself to the next level or to reach a goal. Cultivating focus, strength, willpower, and patience will help you. Thinking like a Ranger can take you there.

You might feel impatient at the idea of developing a vision. But your thoughts matter. Your emotions and behavior will follow from your thoughts, and the clearer you can be about what you want, the easier it will be for you to follow a path to success on your mission. Write down your goals. There is all kinds of scientific research to back up the utility of explicit goal setting and how it helps people focus their time and energy to accomplish tasks and increase their sense of well-being. I know the truth of it in my own life; I need a clear sense of mission to stay on track. Ask yourself:

When I imagine my ideal life, what does it look like?

What are my core beliefs and values?

What do I really want to achieve?

What are my key assets?

What is my mission on this Earth?

What would I do to defend my mission?

Try to silence everyone else's opinions when you think about this. I know that can seem damn near impossible, and of course you're going to make your real-life decisions taking a whole range of real-life responsibilities and obligations into account, but that will come when you start to plan your attack. Right now, just work on getting clear with yourself about what you believe in, what you want to do, and why.

Go ahead and think big. That doesn't mean you won't need to make some short-term objectives and smaller changes on the way. You'll see from my experience that a successful operation depends on sweating the small details. So you'll probably have both short- and long-term missions to tackle. But if you can define those missions in terms of something big, something important and meaningful to you, you'll be more successful. It might be the thing that scares the crap out of you, something you're almost afraid to say out loud. Do it. Be brave and take risks. "Fear not" appears in the Bible hundreds of times; take it for real.

Draw strength, too, from the subgoals you achieve and the tasks that go well. Pay attention to your small victories. I'm not talking about being self-congratulatory over nothing. I've got three little kids, and you don't want to get me started on how I feel about participation trophies in kids' sports today. So, sorry, you won't get kudos from me for showing up. Set your bar high. But do notice as you get stronger and achieve certain milestones on the way to your goal. Give yourself a pat on the back when you achieve a success you worked for. For me that might have been qualifying on a shooting test; for another soldier it might have been running a sub-seven-minute mile. For you it could be getting one car cleaned out front to back, having one day of healthy meals or one week of exercise, or acing a math test on your way to completing whatever larger mission it is you've set yourself.

You may well fail at some tasks, but you can't let that stop you from achieving your mission. Failure is not an indictment of you as a person, it is an experience. When you risk and reach for things, you will fail, over and over. The key is to survive it by picking yourself back up, keeping your eyes on the mission, and continuing to ask for more. If you are a Ranger, your attitude is going to be "I will accomplish this mission or die trying." Literally. This is exemplified by the sixth stanza of the Ranger Creed: "Readily will I display the intestinal fortitude required to fight on to the Ranger objective and complete the mission, though I be the lone survivor." When you believe you can succeed, when you believe you can beat down that voice in your head that is going to tell you you should quit, you will learn that you can bear more pain and accomplish more than you think you can. Give yourself a chance to draw strength from that.

The stakes on a special ops mission are high. Our failure can endanger people, it can cost lives, it can affect our country's strategic position in the world. That is some powerful motivation to complete a mission and get it right. The stakes are high for you, too: you need to have goals that motivate you properly because this is your life. You need to understand your own story to set your mission and become the leader of your life.

Chapter Five

DEVELOP A BATTLE PLAN

Acknowledging the fact that a Ranger is a more elite Soldier who arrives at the cutting edge of battle by land, sea, or air, I accept the fact that as a Ranger my country expects me to move further, faster, and fight harder than any other soldier.
—RANGER CREED

Success in a military operation is all about the due diligence. We need to plan, consider alternate timelines and alternate scenarios, and often coordinate strategies with others. Just to keep it interesting, this usually needs to happen under dynamic conditions. We have to identify and focus like a laser on all the factors we can control because there are always going to be a bunch of things we can't. The worst thing you can do as a planner is waste valuable time and energy stressing about things you can't control. Take it as a given: there will be unexpected contingencies. When they happen, you'll deal with them. You can use planning to make your best guess about what may come up and can then strategize to either avoid possible problems or ready your responses.

Sometimes in the military we call that "to fill and flow." The bottom line for a Ranger is to not quit no matter what happens, so planning needs to be as effective as possible.

The better my planning is, the more informed, logical, and strategic my decisions on the ground will be. Ranger training involves a lot of patrolling, missions to gather information or to conduct combat operations. We learn how to patrol in different climates to try to get a sense, on a physical basis, of the conditions we might face in the field. The more we train, the more confident we're going to be in battle. Once we have set a mission, we are going into battle.

Rangers use core principles of patrolling:

Detailed planning: Make a simple plan, and effectively communicate it to all.

Intelligence gathering (reconnaissance): Confirm what you know, and learn what you do not already know.

Security: Preserve your force as a whole.

Control: Have a clear understanding of the concept of the operation, the commander's intent, and discipline.

Common sense: Use all available information and good judgment to make sound, timely decisions.

As GRS operators providing security in dangerous places, we must keep all of our tactical and technical equipment in good order. We do a lot of training in the United States in high-speed evasive driving, off-road driving, and motorcade operations. Everyone has solid shooting training and has to maintain expert proficiency on all weapons systems carried by GRS operators. Some of the shooting standards are pretty challenging. The timeline I had to meet for shooting particular targets was seconds, and about half the class in the initial GRS vetting course generally failed.

* * *

We did a lot of slow grind work in GRS and a lot of it is classified, so I can't describe it as well as I'd like to, but planning was the priority in all operations. You probably hear the word *operator* and get a very active, aggressive image in your mind. But we are not spending most of our time running around shooting people like you see in the movies. Good operators need to learn a lot of patience and self-control, and their ability to restrain themselves can be critical to the success of a mission. When you react to something too fast or move too early, you can weaken your own position or give the enemy an advantage, depending on the situation.

As a GRS operator, I would ideally like everyone to schedule everything at least a week in advance. Of course that is not reality, and the people you are protecting do a lot of stuff off the cuff. I need to make sure they're going to be okay, but if I'm given only thirty minutes to plan and get ready to go, I can't guarantee that someone is going to be safe. You give me a week, I can feel more confident that you're going to be okay. But GRS guys have got to be able to function either way and with anything in between. The more I prepare, the better I'm going to be able to move on the fly.

Being prepared also helps you take the initiative when you can. In Benghazi, we were good to go five minutes after we got the call. We waited approximately thirty minutes before we rolled out. It is impossible to know for sure, but there is certainly a good chance that if we had rolled out from the get-go, the ambassador wouldn't be dead. Sean wouldn't be dead. Our waiting gave the enemy time to solidify their position and made it more difficult for us to get to the compound. If we had been able to approach during the initial chaos, we might have been able to take advantage of their not yet having control of the situation. They wouldn't even have known we were coming. The stakes are not normally so high, but I always want to be able to take the initiative when possible, and planning helps me do that.

* * *

I arrived in Benghazi at the end of June, about two months before 9/11, as a member of the Global Response Staff. It was not my first time in Libya. I had worked in Tripoli before, in the same capacity, from the previous December through the beginning of March. That's a pretty standard rotation for someone in my job: a few months on, a few months off.

Wherever we are, our job is to protect places, people, or things. We are protection and the quick reaction force for whomever needs help. If something bad happens in a situation, it doesn't matter whether or not you have been assigned to a particular area—you're still going to go. That's what brothers do for each other. And soldiers—Rangers, SEALS, and Marines—are brothers. When we responded to State in Benghazi, it wasn't unusual. I've responded to the US Army in Afghanistan when it got stuck, to the State Department in Iraq when it got stuck, and to other contracting companies when they've been stuck in various areas of operation (AOs). If there's a 911 call and we're there, we're going. I don't know any GRS guys who would refuse that call.

GRS is required to accomplish other tasks that I can't discuss because they are classified. In our job, good planning requires knowing where our assets are both inside and outside a country. Where are the local hospitals and emergency triage units? Which ones are friendly, and what can they do? Who are the militias? Are there any friendly militia members? Is there a Spectre gunship in Italy? Are there troops in Sigonella, in Sicily? Or in Greece? We need to know where our quick-response guys are, because we may be the only paramilitary or military asset in a particular country. I remember talking to the FBI after Benghazi and being asked, "How did you know you had a Spectre gunship when you called for it?" I looked at them as though they had fish growing out of their foreheads. Are you fucking kidding me? What do you think I do? It's my job to know. That's what I have to do every time I go into a country, and the learning curve is extremely short. I have got to know what's going on within forty-eight hours. That's where working with locals comes in.

I need to learn particular tribes and alliances. For example, in Afghanistan, I had to know who was Northern Alliance, the Tajiks: I got to know that many of them were friends. Most Uzbekis were our supporters, but the Pashto, especially down south in Kandahar and then over on the border of Khost, were usually Taliban. In Iraq, at the time I was there, I didn't want to go into Sadr City. During that time, Mansoor District was safer than Sadr City, and Karada was actually okay. In Libya, I knew that the Zintan militia in Tripoli could generally be relied on. In Benghazi, I knew that Ansar al-Sharia and Rafallah al-Sahati were unfriendly and I couldn't go to them with anything. That was typical of the kind of stuff I had to sort out. I had to know where particular camps were, so that if we were in a particular area and they were operating, we knew what areas we could go into and which we had to get out of. And of course we needed to be familiar with the neighborhoods, physically, so that we could move in them quickly if and when we needed to. We needed to be on alert at all times, but as we learned the landscape, there were usually certain areas where we could relax, relatively speaking.

As a member of the GRS, I became well versed in how to do this and it became second nature. Understanding my environment, my assets, and who my bad guys are is a big part of being good at my job. I need to be sensitive to my location. What works in Pakistan might be completely different from what will work in Libya, Yemen, or Afghanistan. I always got to know the clothing, cultures, and customs, and always tried to speak the languages, as best I could. I was never fluent in any of them, but I made sure that I could understand the basics in a country while I was there, like being able to go into a restaurant and order food, that kind of thing. It's respectful and also protective.

Other than jeans, I would try to buy local clothing, like button-down shirts and sunglasses in the local style. I usually just wear tennis shoes or trail running shoes, because I wouldn't blend in as well wearing military boots. Whether I would wear desert camouflage depended on the particular sites or what the op was, but I couldn't in Benghazi. Sometimes I'd wear low-profile armor, basically a little chicken plate. A level-three soft armor like that will stop a 9 mm and shrapnel, but it won't stop a rifle round. But it's something, and if it's tight enough, it doesn't profile a whole lot if I'm wearing it underneath my shirt. Generally out in town, I didn't wear armor. If you're going to get blown up, you're going to get blown up and that chicken plate was so small that if I got shot, chances were I would get injured anyway. I'd wear it if I was in an environment such as Mosul or Kandahar or Khost, even in Kabul at times, but less often in Benghazi.

Conditions in Benghazi itself were pretty typical for our type of work. Electricity was hit or miss, but we had backup generators when it went down. Some places had air-conditioning. Water was shipped in because we couldn't drink most of the local water. There was no real sewer system, and it flooded a lot when it rained, so the sewage contaminated the drinking water. There was very little infrastructure, and trash was everywhere. It felt like there were just fields and fields of plastic garbage bags.

It was hard to drive in traffic there, because if there were traffic laws, they were certainly not enforced. People were clipping u-turns in the middle of the road. There was no signaling, and drivers would stop right in the middle of the interstate where you were going 70 or 80 kilometers an hour. Cars often broke down or were in poor repair, say, with no brake lights or no working lights at all, even at night. There were ten-year-olds driving cars and people stacked three deep on a motorcycle, so even typical traffic was dangerous. A lot of times we were out in soft cars because armored cars don't blend in real well, so some guys got injured just by getting into basic car wrecks.

The militias were everywhere, and they were the law. It was basically like being in a town being run by a bunch of gangs with guns. Everyone seemed to have a gun. It was not safe, by any means. We were out in town every day and saw a lot of petty crime. That was another delicate balance: we wanted to blend in, but we didn't want to give off a vulnerable vibe. Raymond Allen Davis, a GRS operator working in Pakistan in 2011, was leaving an ATM in Lahore and wound up having to kill two men who attempted to rob him, which landed him in a Pakistani prison for more than two months. We need to blend with a persona that is not an easy target; otherwise we're going to get mugged or beaten, because it's lawless there, and that's what happened to Davis.

When I first got to Tripoli, on a different posting, militias were fighting each other every day. It was almost routine to be driving downtown and get caught in the middle of a gunfight. Guys would have grenade fights, literally throw grenades at each other down the middle of the square, just for the hell of it. They would be fighting very small turf battles, typical gang-style fighting. Don't get me wrong, I wasn't getting caught in gunfights or gunfire every day, but it happened often enough that it was a constant possibility. Usually they wouldn't mess with us if we were just driving through, or we would just get off road and let them do their thing.

The tricky part of all of this is that while we're constantly gathering information and getting acclimated, we have to be ready to ramp up real quick. A good GRS operator knows how to go from zero to 100 in seconds. I happened to be wearing shorts on September 11 in Benghazi, and I fought in those shorts all night. My legs got scratched up, but I still say that a piece of denim or nylon is not going to stop a bullet.

SECURITY AND CONTROL

Physical security is always the top priority of a soldier or a GRS operator. Relationships on the bases when we are overseas differ from place to place, but they can get tense because our job, as security, is to keep people safe, while the job of a case officer (CO) is to connect with people and collect intelligence. Our job priorities are different. Their focus, to gather information, sometimes means they want to disregard some of the safety measures that we need to maintain. Let's say they have a relationship with someone local where a meeting has been set up but the other guys have changed the venue at the last minute. We might say, "No, you can't do it this way because it's really unsafe," and they might come back and say, "But this guy won't meet us without doing it this way." Then we might say, "Well, you could be playing into his hand. We don't know what's there because we haven't had time to figure out if that's a safe area, or maybe it's being set up for someone else to do surveillance on you." Normally, the chief of the base decides how to proceed if there is a conflict between contractors and COs, and sometimes they take your advice and sometimes they don't. We might sound paranoid sometimes, but that's our job and the reality is that people are often playing you in those situations because you've offered to pay them for their information. And if somebody else is paying them more money, they're going to go with that and betray you.

My buddies and I used to call it "the Plan." Money was Plan, and we would joke that "The plan is to give them more Plan." That's the plan, to give them more money. Sometimes giving them money resulted in good information, but other times, if we gave them more money they'd just give us what we want to hear. We have been very lucky to get out of certain situations with not much more than old-fashioned luck.

Staying in control of your emotions when you are frustrated is also key. The way our team had learned how to handle ourselves in bad situations was clear in Benghazi. The same guys who could goof and joke with the locals, or go get coffee and watch a soccer match and not feel like we had to look behind us 24/7, could also get right into battle mode when the shit hit the fan. In our line of work, that's a good operator. For the most part, everyone maintained his composure and fought back when he needed to fight.

Guys who are ramped up all the time are not good GRS operators and won't last at the job. I have to be able to go to a restaurant, walk out in town, buy a paper, or order a coffee. If I am ramped up all the time, I'll give myself away. If I'm always looking like I'm ready to get into a fight, the locals will pick that up immediately and know that I am security. At the very least, they'll think that I'm suspicious and they need to watch me. Then I'm no good to anybody; in fact, I'll put everyone else in danger. On the other hand, I can't be so relaxed that when the shit hits the fan I can't flip that switch immediately. I learned that balance on the job. New guys who can't hit the right balance often weed themselves out, either because they get too burnt out or because, if they're the type who is always ramped up, it's not exciting enough for them.

SWEAT THE SMALL STUFF

GRS guys are frequently on standby, which might last thirty minutes or all day. Some bases are really slow, and other bases have us going hard all day, every day. I had basically been on standby all day on September 11 in Benghazi. It was a small enough base that we didn't need to hang out in the team room or the HQ all day. Everyone handles that time differently: some guys read books during downtime, other guys try to get degrees online. Every base has some sort of make-shift workout facility. Sometimes guys play video games or watch TV, if we have one. Local TV can be better than you expect and also helps you learn the language.

We also use our downtime to maintain our proficiency and readiness. We prep our equipment and make sure our mapping software is up to date. Sometimes I would practice shooting or make sure my weapons and gear were good to go so that I could just throw them on when I needed them. We all had go bags at the ready. A go bag can look like any-thing from a camera bag to a little camelback backpack. Our map and compass might be in there and usually some medical equipment. I'd have a quick clotting agent of some type and at least four or five tourniquets, and they were all staged and ready to go. I took them out of their packaging so I could do my own tourniquet with one hand if I had to. In Benghazi, I had a radio to maintain contact with the team and with head-quarters. We also had two lighter machine guns. When we got the call that night, I picked up my go bag and my weapons, and I also grabbed my pistol and took it to the compound. I swung my rifle, grabbed my machine gun and a couple hun-dred extra rounds, and that is all I had, basically a drum and two hundred extra rounds slung around my neck plus my rifle and magazines stuffed into the cargo pockets of my shorts. I was ready in less than five minutes.

Our cars were at the ready on September 11 as well. All the GRS guys would routinely have responsibility for differ-ent maintenance checks and services. If I was on vehicles, for example, I would check all our vehicles regularly, making sure the oil was okay, the tires were pumped, all the cars had brake fluid, that type of thing. If something needed fixing, I'd take them out and get them serviced. We had a local guy to service them, but we would have to stay with him while he was working on the vehicle. In that situation, we're in a heightened state of readiness, so we really do need to be that vigilant about the state of our vehicles.

COMMON SENSE

GRS operators are sometimes treated like a necessary evil by the people we are hired to protect, at least until something bad happens. Relationships are not always contentious, but sometimes there is that edge. I know our night in Benghazi changed some attitudes as far as how some COs look at GRS. In Tripoli, we had two guys who thought they were real-life Jason Bournes and didn't want to take us with them to a meeting. Well, even though those two Treadstones spoke Arabic and were carrying guns, they got themselves hemmed up at a checkpoint and couldn't get out of it. So we got the call: "Help us, we can't get through."

"Roger that, we're on the way."

It didn't matter that they hadn't wanted our help in the first place, we were still going to go. When we got there, we found the two guys sitting in their car with the windows rolled up, staring straight ahead through the front windshield of their locked car. They looked like secret agents in a movie. But the situation did not feel particularly hostile to me. I got out of my car and walked up to the guard, who did not speak English. My Arabic is not good, and I was not sure which militia he was with. I walked up, showed the guard my cover identification, told him that the men were diplomats, that they were with me and good to go. We might have exchanged one or two friendly sentences, but he basically said, "Ok, yes, sir, Americans." And he let them through.

I tried to be nice about it afterward with the COs, but I couldn't help asking "Guys, why didn't you just roll down your windows and talk to them? They run the city, and it's a checkpoint. Sometimes they just want to talk or they want to tell their buddies they talked to an American." Use your common sense. You have got to engage. If you feel they're trying to pull you out of the car, you can pull out your karate moves and do your secret agent stuff.

WISDOM FROM THE RANGERS
PRINCIPLE THREE: PLANNING MAKES YOU ADAPTABLE

You need a battle plan. The principles of patrolling can be applied to your civilian life, and the core principles of patrolling can be applied to any mission. They are not consecutive; as a Ranger, you need to be responsible for all five simultaneously. For example, maybe your mission has to do with getting a particular contract or promotion at work. That is an outcome you can't exactly control. However, you are in control of how much you are willing to learn, train, and experience in areas that will help you reach your goal. What can you do to demonstrate your readiness for the job you want? You might be excellent at your job, but how well do you understand the larger landscape it exists in? Could you perform the jobs of the people above and below you? What skills or certifications do you need, and how can you get them if you don't already have them? Do you understand the larger company and profession you are in (or want to be in) and who your competitors are? Answering those questions is part of your planning.

It's one thing to know the facts and tactics that are relevant to your job or situation; it's another thing to be able to use that information. It is like the difference between reading about a weapon and learning how to shoot it. You have to practice to get proficient. You need to practice harder to get fast and accurate. Do some people take to certain skills more quickly than others? You bet. But you don't know how good you can get at something until you give it your best effort, over and over. Mastering the necessary skills you identified during planning is part of your own recon, and it's a good time to sweat the details.

Sometimes you just don't have the time you'd like in the military, or in life, but you're more likely to have a bit more time and space in the civilian world. So take your time when you can, and be patient. Big changes aren't going to happen overnight. But you can make them happen in the end.

Being prepared is essential to conducting a successful mission. You can be sure that not everything is going to go according to your plan because you simply can't control everything. When unexpected obstacles emerge, your judgment about how to respond and your ability to adapt will be directly related to the quality of your planning. And there is a lot you can control. Drilling a plan will help you evaluate your assets and liabilities, identify potential problems, make you ready to seize the initiative if the opportunity presents itself, and increase your probability of success. The stronger your plan, the more confident you will be as you get ready to attack your mission.

I hope that you don't take your safety for granted, but guess you are usually able to go about your business and your life without having to think too hard about it. You might consider aspects of your security in a larger sense as you devise your battle plan, though: consider if there are possible threats to you or your plan (economic, medical, personal rivalries, weather conditions, anything) and how you might avoid or respond to them.

Keeping control of your mission means you are communicating and coordinating with other people who are involved in it. You must continually drill the mission using all your available assets. As a civilian, your squad might be your family members or your coworkers. Everyone should share an understanding of the larger mission, the battle plan, and his or her role in it.

Staying in control of your emotions is an important practice, too. When you are worried about a deadline, overwhelmed by a seemingly insurmountable pile of papers on your desk, or frustrated by a client, it is easy to lose perspective and take your anger or anxiety out on the people around you. That might be understandable, but it is counterproductive. If you find yourself in an explosive rage, you have almost certainly lost control of your mission.

You might not need to maintain a military level of readiness, but there is no reason you shouldn't develop your own particular list of maintenance checks and use your downtime to take care of them. A lot of people live in a kind of crisis state. You might know what I'm talking about if you have ever been driving on fumes while counting miles tensely on a highway, hoping that a gas station is on the horizon. There are a bunch of basic tasks we all have to do, and many of them can be ignored for a bit, no big deal—until it becomes one. Let's say you wind up driving to a store in the middle of the night to get an ink cartridge for your printer because yours ran out and you need to print something to turn in the next morning. I applaud your willingness to do what it takes to make your deadline, but I'm also not too sympathetic about your drama because, hey, if you'd had an extra ink cartridge on hand, it wouldn't even be a story, right? It's not glamorous, but being attentive to small details and maintaining a general state of readiness will make your life run smoothly. It will free your energy for your bigger mission focus. So keep on top of the daily stuff.

Once you develop a system of planning and preparedness that works for you, try to stick with it in a disciplined, routine way for a few weeks; you need to get yourself into your battle rhythm. Your battle rhythm is going to be your daily grind, your *Groundhog Day*, and, believe it or not, the days are going to feel as if they are flying by as you get closer to your goal.

Use good judgment. Stay flexible. If you have planned well and done your reconnaissance, you will read changes in your situation more accurately and feel more confident when you need to deviate from your plan.

———————————————————

Chapter Six

GET TOUGH

Be . . . Technically and tactically proficient.
—*RANGER HANDBOOK,* "LEADERSHIP," 1–1

One of the positive things that happens in military training is that most everyone improves his fitness. There are physical targets and standards I had to meet to become a member of the 75th Ranger Regiment, and being in peak fitness is a job condition. But you can set your own standards, and they don't need to be those of a Ranger or a professional athlete. When you commit to improving your physical self, the attitude and discipline necessary to do so can expand into other areas of your life. Life will throw all kinds of obstacles, threats, and unknown things at you. You want to develop the mental agility and will to be able to react swiftly and effectively.

* * *

During the first week of Ranger training, we did something called a gazelle run. Eighty or ninety guys were expected to run in formation for five miles, which seemed pretty straight-forward. But the sergeants played a little game with us where one guy would run as hard as he could and crush it for a mile. The leader set the pace, so you had to keep up with him. Then that leader would fall back and another cadre member would come to the front and lead for a mile, and he would max it. We would have to keep up with this rotating cast of leaders for five miles. We were all getting stronger, but we had also been routinely going to bed at about midnight and needed to be up and ready to max that run by 5:30 each morning. I was not intimidated by a five-mile run, but having to keep up with the rotating leaders each crushing it for a mile was a complete mindfuck.

I started in the middle of the pack, but when the sergeant started tearing it up, I felt as if I was trying to catch a rabbit. Guys would fall out and back and then back in again, so the faster runners, including myself, started to weave our way out of formation to get up to the front. There were maybe five of us managing to keep up with the sergeant at what must have been a five-minute-per-mile pace. I remember that three of those guys had been in basic training with me. We were just running as fast as we could, trying to keep up with the rotating cast of leaders and hoping that the formation behind us was holding. At some point, they had us do a U-turn, still running. I remember flipping around and seeing bodies just flung back along the road for about a half mile. It was still pretty dark out because it was so early in the morning, but you could see some guys bent over with their hands on their knees and others literally lying down, gasping for breath. The sergeants started screaming "Catch up!" "Get back in formation!" "You slow ass fat sons of bitches!" "You want to quit? Get in the truck." There was a flatbed following us for those who wanted to quit. A few guys got onto it.

We got back into formation and started the second mile, and it started all over again. I could hear more guys quitting behind me during that second mile, and I think it was because they knew we were facing five of those. They had already given up. I was keeping up but feeling doubtful as I focused on the length of the task. My lungs were burning, and I was wondering if I could possibly keep the pace for five miles. I didn't think I could, but thought, "I'm going to pass out before I drop out." About halfway into the second mile, the sergeant slowed the pace from a five-minute mile to something a little slower. The next three and a half miles gradually slowed and were probably at seven-and-a-half- or eight-minute paces, which were relatively more manageable.

I came to see that, in training at least, the beginning of any exercise was always the hardest. They wanted to see how we would react. But if we could hang on for it, the pace or intensity would eventually lower to something more manageable. They train us that way because they need to see who is going to quit. The purpose of those exercises is not sadism. They need to weed out the quitters because a Ranger simply can't quit on the field. Can the guys who quit still be good soldiers? Absolutely—in some other capacity, but not as a Ranger.

The guys who make it through Ranger training are not necessarily the biggest, strongest, or fastest ones. Though they need to pass tests with stringent standards, it doesn't mean they all necessarily have the best technical skills. But every last one of them is strong enough to endure fear and pain and demonstrate the mental toughness required to stick with the hard training. Someone might have that kind of dedication and find that his physical abilities are not up to par. That's OK. Not everyone can reach the same goal. The point is not for everyone to be a Ranger. The point is that if you know you have done your very best, you can take the knowledge of your current limits, strengths, and weaknesses, as well as the quality of mental toughness, into your recon as you figure out your next move. If you can take that attitude in the face of disappointment or failure, you are getting tough like a Ranger.

Physical training during RIP required endless repetitions of push-ups, sit-ups, mountain climbers, flutter kicks, and other standard calisthenics that were also used throughout the day to punish us as a group for any failure or infraction. There were also routine runs. Sometimes they got more creative: log PT, for example, required us to work as a unit while also providing a workout. As a group, we would each have to put an actual log across our shoulders and do overhead arm presses or run with it. We might do sit-ups with the logs, too, and just about anything else you can imagine. Log PT requires a fair amount of coordination and teamwork in addition to strength, and there are similar exercises in SEAL training.

It's challenging and certainly theatrical looking, but I found it less tough than the endurance required by the running and marching with the rucksacks.

During our first week, we had to do a twelve-mile road march with our rucksacks. We were not allowed to run but required to stay in formation as we walked a fifteen-minute-per-mile pace with a fifty-pound ruck on our backs. If you have never paced yourself, that is very brisk. Guys were falling out left and right, and it became chaotic because people started to run to keep up. That screwed up the guys in the back. We were required to maintain our group formation, so there was an accordion effect, and guys who started jogging instead of marching at the front made the guys at the back have to sprint. I could keep up, but it was frustrating because I couldn't help the other guys. I always want to be positive and be a good team member, but that exercise was not a place where I could grab another guy's ruck for a bit and lighten his load or help push him forward. It was an individual, suck-it-up event. And make no mistake, it does suck, even when you are keeping pace.

We had been doing so much running and walking that everyone had blisters, so most of us were walking through physical pain. They let us wear moleskin, and I remember figuring out how to use it that week and having to prioritize my blisters with the limited amount we were given. Blisters on the backs of the heels are the worst; the ones that develop on the tops and bottoms of your feet are less debilitating. It's a small thing, but anticipating and strategizing about how to deal with that kind of physical pain are an example of problem solving. After a couple of months, my feet got so tough from all the rucking and running that I didn't need the moleskin anymore. I was getting to know my own body, understanding what might hurt, and thinking about how to protect and fix myself. Planning for such contingencies, rather than thinking "I can't do this," is a kind of mental toughness. I also developed toughness by accepting the pain and walking through it the best I could while it was happening. A big old truck followed us on that march, as they often did, and you could climb on if everything got to be too much, but that might get you cut from the program. The RIP cadre riding it would call out, "Get on, softie, there are coffee and doughnuts waiting for you back home." About ten guys dropped out after that first ruck march once they got into the truck.

The Army was not playing a sadistic hazing game with us during those exercises. The physical condition of a Ranger is critical for our battle readiness. The Army needs soldiers to be operating at peak capacity, for their strength, speed, and agility be the best they can possibly be. But being physically strong is only part of the picture, because soldiers may have to make life-or-death decisions under stressful, chaotic conditions. It sucked at the time, but I'm glad I experienced all of the pressure and stress during physical training because it served me well when I needed it in the field. I had felt the pain, the sweat, the heat, the cold, and I knew I could handle it. I believe you will revert back to your highest level of training when you need to, so it will serve you to train and train and train some more.

STANDARD OPERATING PROCEDURE

The routines of military life remove a lot of temptation and choice. Following orders is a kind of discipline, and the standard operating procedures (SOPs) the military uses make it easier to get or stay strong by taking certain choices away. But it is not enough to show up and just follow orders. The guys who really do well in the Army are the ones who develop the self-discipline to go further. The guys who volunteer for additional training, who work to improve their shooting by going to the range on their downtime, or who do do extra PT not just to qualify on their tests but to max them are the guys who distinguish themselves.

THE ATHLETIC MIND-SET

If you ever played sports as a young person, you know what I am talking about. When you are in a situation that requires you to pull everything you can out of yourself, being an athlete gives you a base to draw on. My father was a football coach, so athletics were a big part of our lives growing up. We moved to follow his coaching appointments in Colorado, Oregon, and Utah, so I grew up watching him coach in different environments. My brother and I would hang out at sports facilities, watch practice, and then play football during the game times. I always played competitive sports, mostly Little League baseball, basketball at the

YMCA, and football. I can't remember when I started playing organized football, probably when I was in first grade, but it was my favorite.

In high school, I played varsity football, basketball, track, and baseball. Playing football was an important part of my college experience: I was a junior college All-American wide receiver and was recruited by Brigham Young and South Carolina but chose to return to Mesa State College in Colorado, where my dad was the head football coach and athletic director.

Playing football as a teenager taught me about winning and losing, being a member of a team, listening to an authority figure, performing under pressure, and making small adjustments to strategy. Being pushed to give my very best effort and "leave it all out on the field" had a profound effect on my attitude. Many of the guys I served with in the military had played sports, too. It makes sense, if you think about it, that playing sports would help you prepare to be a soldier, not only in terms of fitness but in your understanding of the role that effort and attitude play in your performance.

I can't compare athletics and military service, and I will never say that college football or baseball, or even professional sports, would prepare you for being in combat. I don't care what any pro athlete says. Physically, maybe, although strength in the military is more about endurance than the sudden power moves you need to make in football. People can train for that, so maybe they can do it, or at least make it part of the way there, on that physical basis. But mentally and emotionally, combat is different because soldiers have to think of more than just themselves. The only time it was ever about me in the military is when I was going through a school and had to pass certain tests, but even some of that evaluation can be based on how I handle myself within a team environment. In sports, for me, it was kind of fifty percent team, fifty percent personal. In the military, especially as part of a special ops unit, it's really about my buddies and making sure they're okay. It's truly not about myself at all. So athletics gave me a base, physically and mentally, but it did not completely prepare me for the military. Nothing can.

TOUGHNESS IS MENTAL

Excelling at sports or improving your fitness is a real head game. Your body is under stress, and you need to will yourself through the pain, up that hill, or to the end of the number of sets and reps you know you can do. You learn that in the military, but you can also feel it when you push yourself physically in civilian life. Your mind can push your body when it wants to quit.

Staying calm and being able to do your job under stress require being mentally tough. A lot has been written about mental toughness, and some of it is very mystical sounding. It's basically about being able to perform no matter what else is going on, no matter what your body is telling you it would rather do and no matter how negative the outcome looks. It's about being able to stay calm, confident, and controlled. That toughness is what is going to help you endure tough training under extreme circumstances. It's your commitment, your willingness to stick with it, that you'll carry with you. Every time you are able to stick with something longer than you thought you could, you get tougher.

HURT VERSUS INJURY

One of the things my football coach dad drilled into me early on was to know the difference between being hurt and being injured. Injury is a broken leg, a badly sprained ankle, or a gunshot wound in the wrong place. An injury messes with your stability, and you'll make it worse if you push through it. In my line of work, many people get injured in one way or another, over and over. It can be incredibly demoralizing not to be able to perform the work you were trained to do because you're recovering from an injury. Hurt is painful, but it's different. I have arthritis in all my fingers now, but I consider that a hurt. I can still shoot, and I can still punch a bag. The hurt you feel from sore muscles after a good workout is a message from your body that you worked hard and are getting stronger. Some kinds of pain can be managed and worked through.

During Ranger training, you expect to have some pain. You're hurting all the time: hurt is normal, hurt is routine, hurt is basic. You learn to accept the pain of hurt and push through it because being in pain is not an excuse to quit. Rangers get goofy with pain, so we embrace the suck: we laugh, we make fun of it, and we try to stay positive. Whenever we were in the middle of a smoke session, we Batt Boys would laugh and ask for more. The more the other guys complained and whined and the more frustrated the RIs got, the funnier it was. It was bravado, but that is how you get through tension and stress. Even if you're faking it, try to go to your happy place, embrace the suck, or make fun of your pain. There is misery in combat, and a Ranger has to learn how to work through it. There is misery in life, and you can, and must, work through yours. Get tough and get started.

WISDOM FROM THE RANGERS
PRINCIPLE FOUR: DISCIPLINE CREATES STRENGTH

When we plan an operation in the military, we talk about our assets. Even if you don't feel your body is an asset right now, you have the power to turn it into one. I don't have to know who you are or what your goals are to know that you will feel better if you make it a point to become physically fit. Becoming, or staying, fit makes you stronger and requires a kind of mental strength and discipline that you can bring to bear on other areas of your life.

When you improve your fitness, it will benefit your health, sleep, concentration, stamina, coordination, confidence, and mood. You don't need to get to your peak fitness in order to see those benefits; even relatively small improvements will help. But there is another dimension to being fit, a benefit that you experience only when you push yourself to your max: you learn how strong you can really be. You need to know your own physical limits in order to make assessments as a leader in a combat situation: what can you handle, what can your guys handle? You know what you can handle only to the extent that you have tested yourself.

Compete with yourself, and push yourself to improve your fitness. Not only will it help you maximize your own potential as an athlete, it will help you understand how strong and disciplined you can be. Improving your fitness will contribute to your resilience, both physical and emotional, so try to create a gradual, but real, increase in what you demand of yourself. That might mean that if you can do ten push-ups today, start shooting for twenty. Or maybe you want to see how you stack up against a member of the infantry. The PT test for Army basic training when I was there required you to perform two minutes of push-ups, two minutes of sit-ups, and a two-mile run. The standards today, which are lower than they used to be, require a twenty-one-year-old guy at the beginning of training to do thirty-five push-ups and forty-seven sit-ups, and he has to complete the two-mile run in 16:36. By the way, that is a bare minimum. There is a more complicated and revised physical fitness test the Army now uses that incorporates a shuttle run, a long jump, and some rowing, and you can look up the standards on all those for your age and gender, if you're interested. Give yourself the same test, and establish your own baseline. Take it from there.

CHOW, RACK OPS, AND EMBRACING THE SUCK

This for sure is not a diet book. I'm not telling you to go on a diet or what kind of diet to go on if you want to, but I know how it feels when I pay attention to what I eat. Food is fuel, and you need to eat properly in order to perform at your best. There doesn't have to be anything precious about it: food in the military is not even called food, it's called "chow," and it's all about calories and nutrition, certainly not about taste. A lot of our rations are highly processed, meant to withstand extreme heat or cold and travel. And as you can imagine, when we get to eat civilian food, it's not generally a four-course Italian meal. I have been in situations where I felt, quickly and directly, what it meant to eat poorly. But you probably don't have that problem as a civilian, and you have a lot of control over what and how you eat. Try making some healthy changes for a few days or a few weeks, and see how you feel.

It does not matter if your ultimate goals are not physical. If you are taking your objectives, and your life, seriously, you need to think about how being in shape will give you a leg up. I'm not talking about driving yourself crazy trying to become an Olympic athlete. You will find that taking care of yourself in basic ways, including eating and drinking properly and moving more, will give you an edge. You'll have more confidence. You'll probably sleep better, too, which is likely to have a positive, direct effect on your mood and stamina. This really has very little to do with how you look, it's about how you feel. Are you breathing a little easier? Do you have more energy? Do you feel tougher? Do you feel more confident?

You might have to slog through some discomfort, or even pain and misery, on your way to finding out how good you can feel. And there might already be misery in your everyday life. Maybe just getting up in the morning and getting to work is a kind of misery for you. You want to work toward adjusting your situation so it doesn't feel that way, but in the meantime, pushing through that misery is critical. At least you're pushing. Ranger training has given me a nice point of comparison when I have felt miserable in my civilian life. I can ask myself: Are you rising before 5:00 a.m. every day and doing two to three hours of intense physical training? Are you having hazing-type games played on you during downtime? Are you being pushed to your physical limits? Are you constantly being yelled at? Usually not, and that puts things into perspective for me. Remind yourself that things could be worse, and try to get comfortable being uncomfortable.

Get tough on yourself, but use common sense. If you're not training to be a Ranger, don't purposefully push yourself to be profoundly sleep- or food-deprived. You don't want to burn out before you begin. Make sure that your standard operating procedures give you periods of recovery, cross-training, and sleep. During Ranger training, we called sleep "rack ops" and felt pretty good if rack ops began by midnight. That didn't happen very often. Take your rack time seriously. And give yourself time to recover, but know that recovery doesn't mean sitting on your butt. Recovery means walking instead of running if your legs are very sore. Recovery means cross-training to give different muscle groups a break: focus on an arm workout the day after one where you focused on your abs, or alternate a strength workout with a cardio workout with a flexibility workout, depending on your goals. There are hundreds of books and online resources that can help you learn how to mix up workouts, and you will figure out what makes sense for you. So go lower intensity if you need to, but keep moving every day and make sure you get your rack.

STANDARD OPERATING PROCEDURES (SOPS)

You want to create personal SOPs that help you pursue your goals, whether that goal is to do fifty push-ups or five. Start where you are. Don't delay putting your SOPs into place: the worst part of any mission is the waiting. Once you start, you'll go into mission mode, and even if it takes you a while to get compliant with your new routines, it's better to start. Maybe you don't have a tabbed spec-4 standing there screaming to make sure you show up and do it or else he is going to smoke you. But there eventually will be consequences for not doing what you need to do in order to accomplish your goal.

SOPs are not only for fitness. You can also identify an area in another, nonphysical, part of your life where you can get tough on yourself. Maybe you want or need to quit drinking or smoking. Maybe there is a list of projects and small repairs you need to do at home that you have been avoiding. Maybe you want to get an A in a class, learn a language or a musical instrument, or improve your shooting. Maybe you want to have a family dinner three nights a week. I don't know what your goal might be, but pick something meaningful to you and get tough with yourself about it. Now, it's possible that you are going to get it done on the first try, but more likely that you won't. If you don't quit and you make a point of paying attention when you fail or get off track, you're already winning because you are going to learn about yourself while you go after that goal.

It might not sound exciting, but routines, practice, and self-discipline are at the core of success for most people in most situations. In the military, we drill on SOPs for a whole range of tasks until they are second nature. In your own life, you need to develop SOPs that promote good habits, and your fitness is a good place to start. The Army requires a lot of repetition of basic exercises. When you stick to a fitness routine, you will develop self-discipline as well as improve your physical performance.

Once you figure out what you want to get good at, you want to be relentless about your practice. And I don't mean just showing up. You've got to refine and perfect your form and then do it again and again. And then you add something new. For a Ranger in combat, a mistake can cost lives, so that was some serious motivation to get our accuracy, speed, strength, and precision as close to perfect as we could. Just as we found in Benghazi, you will be able to draw on all of your practice and experience, almost instinctively, when you are put to the test.

Even though your job may not require you to be in top physical condition, your life will be better if you take charge of your fitness. I'm not saying that you need to train to jump out of a helicopter or even pass the basic training PT test. Start wherever you are. I'm a runner, and I like to encourage people to try running or walking because it's cheap and easy and you'll see improvement quickly. In basic training, we ran every day during PT and were assigned different groups for running, according to our abilities. I was in the fast group, which was initially expected to keep a 6.5- to 7-miles-per-hour pace, and they really do expect you to keep up with the drill sergeant leading the pack. I have always been blessed to be a fast runner, but it was a serious effort to keep it up on top of everything else we were doing. But we ran every day, and even from that starting point, we saw improvement. By the last day of training, we were burning it, and I realized I was right up on the drill sergeant. He waved me ahead saying "Don't wait for me!" I realized afterward that we had been pacing 5.5 miles per hour and I wasn't even tired.

You can time yourself running a mile. If you can't run a mile, walk one and time that. Do so every day or every other day for a week and see how you feel. Just get started. If you don't want to be bothered with a stopwatch or mile tracking (even though you can easily download one on your mobile phone), an alternate approach it is to walk or run for thirty minutes and see how far you get. Repeat that every day or every other day for a week, and see how you feel. Raise the bar and set a new goal for yourself the next week based on how you did. You don't have to train for the Olympics. Maybe you want to add fifteen minutes to your walk next week and work your way up to a 5K. Or maybe a good goal for you is to run one mile without stopping. Know yourself, consult with a doctor, and identify an area of your physical fitness where you can challenge yourself.

Exercise is personal, and goals vary: improving your physical condition can be a question of improving your strength or speed or stamina, or some combination of the three. And if you'd rather bike or lift weights or take workout classes instead of run, knock yourself out. Sometimes it takes a bit of experimenting to figure out what works for you, and it's worth the effort to do that because you'll be more likely to stick with an exercise routine when you enjoy it. I just suggest running because it works well for me and most people surprise themselves with quick improvement when they start doing it and stick to it. But any kind of physical effort that keeps you coming back for more will work. And if you can't find a form of exercise you like right off the bat, do not let yourself off the hook. You know you can keep doing something even when you don't enjoy it, right? Sometimes we do things we don't enjoy because we know they're good for us. You have my permission to embrace the suck. I'm pretty sure that eventually you'll figure out a way to move that you enjoy.

There is no one regimen that works for everyone, just as there is no single physical program for all soldiers after infantry. Everybody needs to be able to march, run, and swim at certain speeds, carrying certain amounts of weight, for specific lengths of time. Certain programs have their own focus. A rifleman in the line at the 75th Ranger Regiment, for instance, would focus his training on endurance, whereas a mortarman would want to focus on building strength.

Whatever you decide to do as far as improving your fitness, the key factor is to push yourself. Your body will let you know when you're really challenging yourself, and you'll learn what you can handle. By maxing on your physical training you will achieve two things: (1) you'll be in better shape, which will have a positive ripple effect on many other areas of your life, from your confidence to your sleeping patterns, and (2) if you really push yourself, you will see right away that your mind will always be willing to quit before your body will. Every time you power through that feeling and keep going, you get stronger mentally.

Chapter Seven

NEVER QUIT

Surrender is not a Ranger word.
—RANGER CREED

've been in plenty of situations that have seemed impossible, where it would have seemed to make sense to retreat or abort a mission. But my father always told me that once you start something, you have to finish it. And Ranger School teaches soldiers to endure a situation even when it seems that there might be justification to quit. Yes, it is designed to teach us how to patrol, to navigate, to do mountaineering and swamp operations, but the larger goal is to teach us how to perform at our very best under extreme circumstances, when we are exhausted, frustrated, stressed, and angry. Special ops training is designed to try to make guys quit because we can't have a quitter in a firefight, and I know we saw the result of that training in Benghazi.

Never quitting isn't the same thing as never failing. Things will not always go according to plan. Rangers and other special operators take it for granted that we are going to encounter obstacles. That's why we rehearse our missions with different contingency plans, because we can be one hundred percent sure that something will not go the way we hoped and planned. We are required to do everything and anything we can in order to complete our mission. That is the bottom line, even if the odds are against us and we might die. In some situations, that means we are literally being asked to fight to the death.

I have learned my lessons about failing and never quitting the hard way, and it didn't happen during a training exercise. Way back when I was playing football at Dixie State Junior College in St. George, Utah, a buddy of mine introduced me to a sweet girl named Susan. I'd like to say it was love at first sight or like being hit by a thunderbolt, but our beginning was far less dramatic than our ending turned out to be. I just hit it off with this kind, beautiful girl and that was it, we were always together. When it was time for me to move to a four-year school to complete my degree, I decided to do it back home at Mesa State College in Grand Junction, Colorado. My father had become the athletic director at Mesa State, which is now known as Colorado Mesa University, and he got me excited about playing for its football team. Susan and I were in love and wanted to move to Grand Junction together, but Susan came from a strong Mormon family and her parents wouldn't let her move with me unless we were getting married. We thought we were right together and didn't want to part, so we moved to Grand Junction and got married. She was nineteen and I was twenty.

My young wife and I shared some very good times together in St. George and Grand Junction. We didn't have a lot of money, but we didn't have a lot of responsibilities, either, and we both had scholarships. But when I graduated from Mesa and wanted to join the Army, we had our first serious, sustained disagreement about our future. Susan did not want me to go into the service, she wanted to finish college, and she did not want me to leave to go into the Army to become a Ranger. I felt sure that joining the military would be a good move. We are both pretty stubborn, and we were navigating a complicated situation as best we could, which is to say, poorly. We finally agreed that I would go to basic training. She wasn't happy about it, but I thought she would eventually join me once I was allowed to live off post.

I had been very confident about my decision to enlist when I was arguing about it with my wife, but I felt apprehensive once I was on the bus to Fort Benning, Georgia. Anticipation is the worst. After about a week of processing, we flew into Atlanta, were picked up in a bus, and rode to Columbus, feeling a sense of excitement and dread. It was really happening. Everyone was still in civilian clothes, no one had eaten, and it was late by the time we arrived. We were met by an intimidating, forceful drill sergeant, who told us to hurry up and wait at attention for the chow hall doors to open. I stared straight at the back of the guy's head in front of me, afraid to move my eyes. We stood at attention for thirty minutes in front of those closed doors. I encourage you to try to standing at attention for thirty minutes. If you would rather just take my word for it, it sucks. It was late, we were tired, and I remember thinking "I hate this." But I did it, and without even realizing it, I was starting to figure out how to zone out so that physical discomfort just disappeared.

They had us stand at attention like that on purpose. It's not as though they hadn't known we were coming. I don't know that anyone really understands at that moment in basic training that he or she has the option to quit, and no one did. Everybody was scared, and everybody stayed still. We would come to find that standing at attention is a common form of punishment in basic. After chow, they sent us back to our bunks and told us to unpack and be ready to be up at 5:00 a.m. We got busy, and I began to focus on what was in front of me. I missed my family, but I wanted to be right where I was.

When I was finally allowed to make a phone call home, I couldn't get ahold of my wife so I called my parents instead. That hurt. A few weeks later, she sent me a "Dear John" letter that basically said, "Hey, I love you, but I don't want to be with you anymore." I remember standing there and reading that letter several times. Even though we had argued before I left and hadn't been able to talk much during training, I was stunned. I believed that when you got married, you stayed married, no matter what happened. I requested permission from my drill sergeant to call my wife, and he gave it to me. When she took my call and told me that she was serious, I physically collapsed and fell to my knees, still holding the receiver of the pay phone. I was broken.

I had done well in basic and was scheduled to take a standardized written test for Officer Candidate School the next day. The questions on the paper swam in front of me that morning, and I felt as though I was living a version of that classic nightmare scenario of having to take a final exam in a course you didn't know you were registered for. My mind was consumed with thoughts of home, and I couldn't remember anything. When I walked out, I knew I had bombed it. That failure derailed the confidence I had been developing during basic. I did become an officer in the Army later, when I went back in the second time, but that's another story.

Toward the end of basic, we spent a week doing field training exercises (FTX) out on a big range at Fort Benning. We had to build fighting positions and set up a safe patrol base where we lived out in the field. We couldn't set up a tent or anything that would give away our position, because other platoons could attack us, so we were all living in a field in little two-man tarps or just sleeping out in the open. The sleeping conditions didn't really matter because every other guy had to be up and awake in case of attack, so no one slept much that week. We would be graded pass/fail as a platoon and I was assigned to be the platoon guide, so I was trying hard to keep it together and lead effectively while struggling with the deepest sense of failure I had ever known. We passed and I was hanging in there, but it was costing me. By the way, I would come to learn that the FTX, or "SuckX," as we called it, was nothing. Ranger School is worse. Real combat is worse. But this was difficult, and I felt tough and proud when we came in and had survived it. I felt like a soldier. Sometimes I would think about the strengths I was developing or the tests I was passing as being bricks in a wall. When I think about that time now, I know that the mortar between those bricks was starting to crack.

* * *

My wife and I had developed a fragile truce, and she had backed off her threat to leave me, but I was in serious denial about the state of our marriage as I focused on completing Airborne Training and RIP. When I graduated from RIP in October 1995, I had about a week before I had to report to my duty station at the headquarters of the 2nd Ranger Battalion at Fort Lewis, Washington. I went home to Grand Junction and continued to refuse to accept the reality that my marriage was not in good shape. My wife was no longer threatening to leave, but she also wasn't home often, even though we had only a week together. But I wasn't going to quit. I felt cautiously optimistic that we were going to power through our problems and that she would eventually come to join me at Fort Lewis. But I felt uneasy as I loaded up my old Toyota Corolla, and I remember driving away from Grand Junction with the unfamiliar sensation of just wanting to drive off the side of the road. I felt sick to my stomach and found myself wondering what would happen if I just slammed into a tree. It was a sense of dread that was new to me, and I kept telling myself "No, this is not right. You need to finish what you started. Let's just get there."

I was unsettled by the state of my marriage, and I was also nervous about how I would be treated as an untabbed private in Ranger Battalion. I had heard stories about how new guys got treated. We had graduated from RIP, but there would be more emotional strain and pain to go through as we continued to try to prove ourselves. We were still going to be pushed and vetted, we were going to get the worst work details, and we would be on CQ or desk duty during our off time. I was intimidated thinking about it and felt I had already had a good taste of what was coming, so I knew it would hurt and that I was not at my best. But I kept thinking "Let's get through the next mile, then the next city." That's the way I got to Fort Lewis, mile by mile. My instincts turned out to be accurate and my troubles were far from over, but I had to wade in and get started. Sometimes that's all you can do, just inch forward and make it through the next mile. You need to continue to move forward, because stopping makes it hard to recover. I was about to find that out, too.

I reported to HQ and was assigned to my company and introduced to my squad. We spent the weekend getting oriented, and gathering and preparing our gear so that it was functional and ready to go. I also found an apartment in nearby Tacoma, thinking that my wife could move in there eventually. As a private, I was supposed to live in the barracks, but exceptions were made for married soldiers. That was a mistake. I should have lived in the barracks because I would have had a support structure after work. Even though we were all miserable, misery loves company and I could have bonded with my unit, even if it was just over the fact that we were all sucking together.

The full battalion came in Monday morning, and we took our PT test. I maxed mine, which felt like a big deal. I loved that about Ranger Battalion. As a private, a lot of what I was graded on was very objective and straightforward: How well did I shoot? How fast did I run? It was a good start for me and a bit of a boost after my initial trepidation, but I could feel that I wasn't emotionally all the way there. I was still working, fast roping out of helicopters and perfecting my jumping and shooting, but every day for the next seven months, I struggled to get up. I didn't want to be there.

Working at Ranger Battalion during that period is how I know what I'm talking about when I say that I get what it's like to have to report to work when you feel down. Every day I wanted to quit, but I was still learning what being a Ranger is about. I fantasized about going home, where I imagined I could work on my marriage and make it right. In retrospect, I understand that there was really no hope at that point because you simply can't control someone else's feelings and Susan's were pretty set. But I had not accepted that and did not want to face what felt like a failure.

I tried to feel cautiously optimistic about my marriage, but, with one excuse after another, Susan didn't come. I had an ongoing sense of dread, but I was also always dog tired, so I was trying not to think about it too hard. Being a private in a Ranger battalion is not a fun experience. It's a great experience, but it's not fun. Privates basically get fucked with every day just because they are privates. That's what happens. I had been warned that being an untabbed private in Ranger Battalion was harsh, and that turned out to be an understatement. Ranger Battalion is not a training environment where the drill sergeants are trying to stress recruits on purpose. The guys in charge of us in Ranger Battalion were generally kids with some power who were physically punishing us or demeaning us because they could, because we were privates. They would make us do push-ups with our feet elevated on the wall, which, if you've never tried it, makes everyone look like a jackass because it is so hard to keep from sliding down. Or, if we messed something up, they might make us duckwalk up and down the hallway. If you want to know what that feels like, you can try it sometime: squat down on your toes with your hands on your head, and walk up and down a hallway for thirty minutes.

Sometimes they made us play Space Invaders, which is a game where the privates dress in Ranger body armor, including our Kevlar helmets, full elbow and knee pads and flight gloves, and our churched-up version of shop goggles. Once everyone was suited up and lumbering around in all that heavy gear, the tabbed Rangers would give us a few trash can lids to use as shields and call us into the hallways of the barracks, which were about three or four feet wide. Then the fun times began as they laughed and threw glass bottles or full cans of soda and beer at us. I wasn't thinking about anything except dodging, but if I'd had a thought, it would have been "Did I really join for this shit?"

The Ranger Battalion is different now. If someone were caught playing Space Invaders, it would be at least an Article 15 violation, a criminal act under the Uniform Code of Military Justice. It might be hard to imagine, but I'm glad that I went through that. It didn't have the same purpose as the smoking I had gotten in basic or RIP training, and it definitely contributed to my stress and anxiety. But it made me feel I could handle some shit. I have never worried about getting into fights or trouble overseas because I know how to handle bullshit, and part of the credit belongs to my experience as an untabbed private in the regiment. So it wound up being worth something, but I was miserable while it was happening.

Meanwhile, I exacerbated a double hernia that I had developed during a jump in Airborne School. The hernias were a bona fide injury and had begun to interfere with my ability to work. I was cleared to participate in a joint readiness exercise at Fort Bragg, North Carolina, with other special ops units that did not involve jumping. I reported for it in a very feisty mood. We were supposed to zero out our weapons during those exercises, but that day I could not be bothered. I just said "Screw it." When my drill sergeant noticed, he went crazy and smoked me up. I did push-ups until I almost passed out, but I can handle that kind of pain. I deserved it. You can't say "Screw it" in the field because you could get someone killed. In that sort of environment, it's like quitting, and it doesn't affect only the quitter. I might have been going through hell, but I had to be there for my teammates. I learned my lesson, but I still didn't know what I was going to do about my personal life.

I was a broken Ranger, away from home, worried about my marriage, doubting my professional readiness, in a constant state of now-familiar physical pain from Ranger training, and going home each night to an empty apartment. I wasn't cleared to do certain jumps and drops until my hernia healed. We were scheduled to do a couple big training exercises with SEAL Team 6 Delta that involved jumping into Fort Bragg, doing some movements, and securing an airfield. It was a cool training op, and I was pissed about having to sit it out. I did desk work while my unit was jumping and called my brother to check in during a moment of downtime. He told me that he thought my wife might be involved with another man. I had considered that possibility, so it was not the same sort of stunned blindsiding I'd felt when I'd received her letter during basic training. But I was devastated.

* * *

My unit was scheduled for a block leave in December and I returned home to Grand Junction, where I confirmed my wife's desire to end our marriage. I was beside myself. I had never met the man who, I thought in that moment, could be helping to destroy my marriage, but I knew his name.

One night, after having a few drinks, I drove out toward the man's house in a cold rage. When I reflect on that night, I view it as a moment of great weakness. I was seriously considering doing wrong. I also see it as a moment of divine intervention, when God did not let me take that easy wrong. This guy lived out in an area full of new subdivisions, and the town was still laying roads. It was a warmish December, and as I navigated the muddy bogs of melting snow, my truck got stuck in the mud. As I sat there, literally spinning my wheels, I thought about having to explain myself to someone if I needed help. I eventually maneuvered my way out of the mud with the four-wheel drive, but it took some time. The interruption allowed me to collect myself and think about what I was doing and what kind of person I wanted to be. I turned around and drove back home. Who knows what would have happened if I had not been forced to stop and think. Would we have fought? Would one of us have injured the other? I don't know.

When I got home, I was overwhelmed and just sat, continuing to drink and sort through my dark thoughts. In hindsight, when I think about getting stuck and then turning my truck around, I see it as a blessing. But it didn't feel like a blessing that night. Actually, even though I knew I had made the right decision, a part of me felt I had chickened out. It was another failure: I had failed at my attempt to take revenge on the man I thought was ruining my marriage. I began to swallow handfuls of Tylenol in between shots of Jack Daniel's. I'm not sure how much I swallowed, but I know it was a whole lot of both. Then I started to feel stupid and sick.

I picked up the phone and called Matt Selcke. Matt had graduated from high school with me, and we had joined the Army together. He'd gone on to Officer Candidate School and I had gone off to Ranger Battalion, but I knew he was also home on leave that night. I called him and said, "Hey, man, you probably need to come and get me."

"What did you do?" he asked.

"I probably need to go to the hospital," I told him. "I've been drinking all night, and I just took a bunch of pills. I don't feel so good."

I don't actually know how long it took Matt to get to me, but it felt like thirty seconds. *Bam*, there he was.

Most people have at least one person in their life they can rely on, someone who will be there no matter what, even if you haven't spoken in a while. The military is full of guys like that, particularly in the special ops community. Matt is special, but I know there are other guys I have served with whom I could call, or who could call me, and we'd be there for each other, no questions asked.

Matt took me to a local community hospital and he also called my dad, who had been our football coach in Grand Junction. When Matt told me he had called my parents, I felt bad but, in my altered state, wasn't sure that this was such a big deal either. I mean, I had taken Tylenol, right? How bad could that be? I told the doctor that I wasn't sure how much I had taken, that I'd just kept eating Tylenol four or so at a time from the bottle, maybe between fifty and a hundred, I couldn't say. The doctors told me that my kidneys could be in danger of shutting down. The next thing I knew, I was drinking charcoal and getting my stomach pumped. And it was starting to feel like a big deal. The doctors had me speak to a psychiatrist from Grand Junction named Dr. Sammons. He suggested that I go to the local VA hospital for evaluation before reporting back to the base.

I wound up staying in the VA hospital for five days. There were a lot of Vietnam veterans during my stay, who were kind to me and made me feel good about having made the 75th Ranger Regiment. I have tremendous respect for those guys, both for what so many of them went through in combat and for the lack of respect they received when they returned home. I was also sobered by seeing how hard some guys were struggling with their issues, even though their military service was years behind them. It was healing to be with them. But I was also growing anxious. I knew that I had really messed up and was worried that there was no way I was going to be able to stay at Battalion. A suicide attempt can get you kicked out of the military. I still wasn't sure if that was exactly what I had been consciously trying to do, but I wasn't at all sure that I'd still have my job when I got back. And I still did not want to quit: I was sorting through my feelings about my marriage and whether or not it could be salvaged.

I was so nervous when I went back to Fort Lewis a week later. I felt everyone would know what I had done and that they would think I was weak and worthless. I reported to my leaders, First Sergeant Grippe and Captain LaCamera. They were decorated warriors, and I was a private. I wasn't sure that they even knew who I was. But both men demonstrated a lot of care and leadership. I remember their attitude was kind of "Damn it, Ranger, why didn't you say something?"

It didn't feel as though they were blaming or berating me. If anything, they seemed disappointed in a missed opportunity, as though they would have liked to have helped me get through it. They encouraged me to return to work, move onto the base, and begin seeing a counselor at Madigan Army Medical Center.

I gave up my apartment and moved into the barracks, where I was surrounded by people. It was good to stay connected to positive people and gave me less time to take deep dives into my own mind games. It turned out that many guys understood what I was dealing with, because troubled marriages are common among Rangers and in the special operations community. That was news to me at the time, but it shouldn't have been. Don't get me wrong, my unit did not transform into a consciousness-raising group, but I got a lot of "We got you, suck it up, you can do this" and appreciated the camaraderie. I began to feel very upbeat and hopeful.

Then I made another bad decision. I was still talking to my wife every once in a while. Looking back on it, I should have cut ties when I returned to Fort Lewis, but we were still married and sometimes we spoke. During one of those conversations, I asked her, "If I left Second Battalion and came home, do you think we could work this out?" I understood her to say yes.

I already had a meeting scheduled with my leaders to determine how to proceed with my service. Captain LaCamera called me into his office with First Sergeant Grippe. They had my counseling reports and the reports from my supervisors spread across the desk. Captain LaCamera looked up at me and said, "If you want to stay, we can keep you in the military. We can keep you in battalion, keep you in your squad, and you'll continue to live in the barracks. If you want to leave, we can put you out with an honorable discharge, but we'll have to do so with a code for a personality disorder, the inability to adjust to military life. Understand that if you ever want to come back in, that will make it harder, even with the honorable discharge."

I remember standing in front of the desk and taking a deep breath before I said, "Sir, I think I want to go home and work on my marriage." I held my breath.

"Yup." Sergeant Grippe looked at me, nodded, and walked out of the office. I sensed that he thought I was making the wrong decision, but he didn't try to talk me out of it. And I'm not sure he could have, even though of course he was right. But sometimes you just have to burn your hand on the hot stove to learn to keep away from it. Captain LaCamera did not really try to argue with me either. He said, "Roger that," and began to explain what would be involved in my outprocessing.

I went home in uniform, with my beret on. I walked into our apartment and took a knee, saying "Please forgive me, please let's stay married." Susan started crying. She said, "I can't stay with you." And that was that. I had been continuously trying to get her to love me again and stay in the marriage. I finally accepted that you can't change someone else's free will. Our divorce was uncomplicated, because we had no assets. Susan and I were too young to be married and I share responsibility for the failure of our relationship. I remember thinking "What did I just do?"

I think I was kind of shell-shocked for a couple of months. I had walked away from a great job, and my marriage was ending. I was a quitter. A double quitter, even. My experience living around friends in the barracks had shown me how important it was to keep from being isolated. So I moved in with two old football buddies, who were excellent company. Maybe too excellent, because without the structure and discipline of military life, I began to drink more. I had met a nurse during my short stay at the VA hospital who turned into a friend when I returned home, which made me feel better; attractive, even, and like less of a loser. That helped a little. Between leaving Ranger Battalion, having the marriage fail, and having my wife cheat on me, I felt like a loser. My whole life felt like a catastrophe. I was trying not to go off the deep end again, but I was completely lost, in a kind of purgatory. The consequences of having walked away from Ranger Battalion began to sink in.

We were still college-aged, and my buddies wanted me to come with them to South Padre Island on the coast of Texas on spring break. I didn't have any money, but they said they couldn't stand to see me so low and offered to pay for me. I went. There was something about changing the scenery that week that helped me start to bounce back. It was sunny and warm, and I felt myself having fun for the first time in a long time. That week, I actually met the woman who would become my second wife. Nothing romantic happened between us then, she just seemed like a cool friend. By the middle of the week, I felt my mood lifting. I remember waking up early one morning and looking out the window at the Gulf of Mexico, watching the sun rise, smelling the salt air, and knowing that I had to keep moving forward.

I was going to have to wait at least two years before I could try to reenter the military, but I thought, that morning, that maybe I would want to do it. And I thought about going to graduate school while I considered it. I felt a happy pulse in my body as I started to envision a plan that would help me make a move to go back where I belonged. If I held on to this clarity of purpose, I knew I was going to complete my mission, even if I had to do it the hard way. Maybe I hadn't quit yet.

I can analyze all the factors that led to my bad decision (and, believe me, I've logged some time with mental health professionals doing just that), but the bottom line is that I take responsibility for my bad decisions. I made decisions that contributed to the failure of my marriage to Susan. I quit the Rangers. They were my bad decisions. No excuses. I was not as strong as I believed I was. I live with it. I created a solution, I paid the price, and, though I might have done it the hard way, I did not stop going after my goal. Every day was a struggle. I was lucky to have strong faith and a supportive family. I was able to hold my dad's voice in my head, telling me to finish what I'd started. That divorce was one of the worst experiences of my life, but in the end it helped me, because it gave me my first taste of real adversity. I forced myself out of that situation by moving and picking myself up by my bootstraps. I got my master's degree, went back into the service, and eventually remarried. But it was tough. And it was embarrassing at Ranger Battalion because I had been doing really well, and then all of a sudden I just fell on my face. It was a deeply humbling experience.

WISDOM FROM THE RANGERS

PRINCIPLE FIVE: NEVER QUIT, EVEN WHEN YOU FAIL

Whatever your goal is, if it is truly challenging and worthwhile, there will be opportunities for you to abandon it and plenty of excuses to quit. Maybe some of those excuses will even be good ones. If it were easy, it wouldn't be much of a goal, right? Because pretty much everyone would have it or do it. No one is tempted to quit when things are going well. But things will not always go well, and you won't know what you are capable of if you give up. So whatever unpleasant or uncomfortable suck factor is in front of you—whatever pressure, stress, or temptation you're dealing with—you've got to see it as a gift. It is an opportunity to see how strong you are. Endurance is the essential quality you need to cultivate in yourself, because it powers everything else.

I have made some world-class mistakes. I've messed up and learned from it. If you mess up, you are going to need to deal with whatever challenges your failure has just created. You have to see it as a chance to create a new goal and an opportunity to learn something and become stronger. Never quitting means you will turn your negatives into opportunities and positives. No matter how badly you have screwed up, you still have resources, or the ability to develop resources, to change direction. Your limits are wider than you think, as long as you never quit. So try to shift gears when life throws down obstacles in your path. Assume that you will encounter tough times, and consider how, not if, you are going to beat them.

Sometimes you will fail. When something goes wrong, you need to be able to rebound as though you're on fire. Being able to recover and adapt to the unexpected is your secret weapon, and it's as important as your technical skills. When things go wrong, some guys will sit in their little sewing circles and complain. Not you, not if you want to win. You are not going to waste your valuable time being distracted or disgusted or feeling sorry for yourself. When you feel bad, go fix whatever needs to be fixed. Even if it breaks some eggs, just go get it fixed. The Army teaches that, and RIP takes it to the next level.

But I can only tell you my story; I can't make you take responsibility for your own life. No one can do that except you.

Chapter Eight

BE ACCOUNTABLE

Seek responsibility and take responsibility for your actions;
exercise initiative; demonstrate resourcefulness; and take
advantage of opportunities on the battlefield that will lead
you to victory; accept fair criticism, and take corrective
actions for your mistakes.

—*RANGER HANDBOOK*, "LEADERSHIP," 1–1

Once I recognized that it had been a colossal mistake to quit the Ranger Regiment, I knew I had my work cut out for me if I was going to be able to fight my way back. That clarity allowed me to set a new goal. I would have to wait at least two years to go back into the military, if it would even have me. But I was determined to resume my path, even though I had made it harder for myself.

Ranger School teaches us to be solution-oriented when something goes wrong, which means we have to analyze what failed and how to correct it. "No excuses" is a core principle drilled into us at Ranger School. There might be legitimate reasons that a mission failed or someone didn't get a promotion or an account. But each person needs to accept responsibility for the failure, period, and take action to move forward.

* * *

The action I decided to take was to go back to school. My parents are both educators. My mom is an elementary school teacher, and my father, who has a PhD, had been a coach and athletic director in high schools and colleges. Their example helped me to decide to take the GRE and apply to graduate school to study criminal justice. That was a subgoal within my larger mission to return to the Army and finish what I had started. As I began to pursue my goal, I reordered my life. I did not date. I did not drink or go to parties. My time was devoted to working, saving my money, studying for the GRE, and doing research about graduate programs.

I wanted to make a fresh start in every way and decided to attend the University of Nebraska at Omaha. Moving away from a place you know can be risky, and I was leaving my family and some good friends behind. But sometimes you need to remove yourself from a problematic situation. I knew one person in Omaha: Tanya, the woman I had met in Texas who would eventually become my second wife. She was still more than a friend, a very sweet woman, and did not blink when I asked her to help me find a place to live with a housing budget of $150 a month. She hooked me up with an eccentric Omaha native who designed and built furniture and rented out rooms in his house. I moved into a room next door to a graduate student from Thailand and started over, with the clothes on my back, a futon, and a fan.

Simplifying your life in a material way can be a great gift, and so can work. When I moved to Omaha, I really had very little. I did have my family, but I did not ask them for anything and lived on what I earned. Many of us want so much more stuff than we need and don't realize how much it can complicate our lives. Simplifying my life helped me clarify and focus. Supporting myself gave me confidence and satisfaction. During that first year in Omaha, I took jobs as a bricklayer, a telemarketer, and a night security guard. Between work and school, I didn't have much free time, but I was working out at the gym at school and feeling healthy. Some of those jobs felt like a pin in my pride after being a Ranger, but I was doing honest work, supporting myself, and starting to feel good. I had been humbled, but I wasn't feeling sorry for myself. I was paying my bills, doing well in my classes, and pursuing a goal, so I was living with purpose. But I struggled with the nagging sense of not having finished what I'd started, and a strategy for returning to the 75th Ranger Regiment was continuing to take shape in my mind.

The goal of getting to Ranger School began to drive what I was doing at the gym. Working out was something I could control. I understood what I might be getting myself back into, so I began to train with the goal of returning to the regiment and passing Ranger School. I knew I could survive the mind games because I had already done it once before. And I wanted to be in peak physical condition, so that I could kill those tests. I designed all of my workouts on the PT standards that would be waiting for me, so I was working to do 120 sit-ups in two minutes, do 120 push-ups in two minutes, and run two miles in eleven minutes and thirty seconds. Anytime I wasn't working or studying, I pushed to do more at the gym. I passed up a lot of parties and did a lot of running. Every Friday night, I would put weight into an old rucksack I'd bought from an Army surplus store, put it on, and do a long ruck run. As I ran, I would visualize crushing those PT tests.

My classes were going well and Tanya and I were starting to grow closer and more serious about our relationship. I was getting into a flow. I would get my homework done, get my workout in, go to class, go to work on the night shift, come home, get some sleep, and do it all over again. I was creating my own battle rhythm. As I already knew from RIP, the body can get used to anything. It got easier as I adjusted to the routine. Many people get impatient and don't push through whatever discomfort or pain or boredom they experience during an initial transition. I accepted that that was how my life was going to be for however long it needed to be, and I got used to it.

Routines helped order my attention and calmed my mind. Every class completed, every second shaved off my mile time, every little bit of improvement felt like a step up. The next year, I moved out of the shared house to my own little apartment. I do mean little: it was about ten by ten, but it was all mine and had an air conditioner. My relationship with Tanya was continuing, and I thought I might be falling in love. I could feel myself changing, becoming stronger and calmer. Sometimes I would sit on my porch late at night after a run and just look around. Omaha is beautiful at night. The head-quarters of Mutual of Omaha were near my apartment, and I could see the lights of its famous sign glowing in the sky. I can remember feeling a sense of gratitude rising in me like a physical force while the rhythm of my heartbeat slowed as I cooled down from the run. Everything that had happened to me in Grand Junction seemed a million miles away. I might have been living in a tiny apartment in a lower-income neigh-borhood, beat tired, and still humbled. But I felt a deep sense of peace and optimism as I sat out on those nights, looking at the lights of those Mutual of Omaha buildings. I was creating some forward momentum in my life, and I could feel it.

Mutual of Omaha was hiring night security guards that first summer, and I applied for the job, figuring it would be convenient because it was so close to where I lived. After a few months, I noticed it had job openings for insurance adjust-ers. It was a salaried position, with benefits, and the company would provide training. A nine-to-five workday would make it more complicated for me to schedule my classes, but I was more than halfway done with school and thought the benefits could be worth the trade-off.

Working in the insurance industry was an unlikely, and illuminating, turn. My supervisor, Scott Holmes, was a for-mer JAG (Judge Advocate General's Corps) officer who understood the ways military training translates into civil-ian life. Scott's training methods were very nonconfrontational, which was a new style of learning for me. I found myself energized as I learned about the business of adjusting, insurance policies, and principles of housing construction and building. Learning something new is invigorating: it makes you smarter, gives you new resources, and expands your horizons. We tend to forget that when we get entrenched in routines. I am still a well-versed senior flood adjuster and occasionally wonder if maybe I'll get back to it someday in retirement.

My experiences in basic and RIP had a direct benefit in my new workplace. I was placed on a team being supervised by a guy named Jerry Dubiak, who was incredibly knowledgeable but also very grouchy. Jerry was an Air Force Vietnam veteran who came by his management style honestly, by temperament and training. The other guys on our team were intimidated by his gruff manner, but after my military training, his temper was nothing to me. I respected his knowledge and accepted his style of leadership, and he's still a friend to this day.

* * *

As I got closer to completing my master's degree, I was also getting closer to the end of the mandatory two-year waiting period before I could try to return to the military. Getting my Ranger tab still felt like my goal. I had studied my discharge papers and was trying to strategize my reentry. I had received an Honorable Discharge but my military Reenlistment Eligibility Code was 3 (RE-3), which meant that I was eligible for reenlistment but would require a waiver in order to do so. I couldn't just sign up again. During my last semester of graduate school, I went to a recruiting station in Omaha for the first time. I handed my papers to the recruiter. I watched him look thought my papers, and my heart sank as his eyes got wide. He looked up at me quickly, and I read his expression to be "Holy crap, are you kidding me?" He noted that RE-3 is code for a personality disorder and said, "Normally this is for guys who didn't make it through basic, but you did. Did you have issues adjusting to military life?" I explained that I had gotten through to Ranger Battalion and told him my story. He was very professional but skeptical, and I felt like a felon. He explained the steps he thought I would have to take but he was not encouraging, and I could tell he thought my reenlistment was unlikely. I was frustrated and humbled but not deterred. I had to keep trying. I figured I needed to talk to different recruiters and see if I could find one with some more room or sympathy.

I continued to approach different recruiters over the next few months while I worked and studied. My application would require extra work and time, and I knew some recruiters would find me unappealing on that basis. When I tried the main recruiting station in Omaha, about three months later, a sergeant major happened to be there. I approached him and said, "Listen, I'd like to tell you my story. I'd like to tell you what happened to me and what I've been doing for the last few years and how much I want to be back in the Army. I know you need guys. I want to be there. I'm a good soldier. I want to go back in, and I will do anything you tell me I need to do in order to go back."

I'd met the right person. He reviewed my paperwork and told me I would need a psychiatrist to confirm that I was ready to return and that I was going to be able to handle being back in the military. He gave me contact information for some local psychiatrists and said I could see anyone I wanted to, private or military.

When I first started seeing a psychiatrist, I felt uncomfortable. Undertaking some honest self-reflection and discussing it with a stranger can be intimidating. And I felt that there was still some stigma around seeing a psychiatrist, that some people still think it might make me sound crazy. (Of course, maybe I am a little crazy to want to do the things I like to do.) It was also a time-consuming process. I had multiple sessions, explaining my background, telling my story, exploring my motivations, and describing what I had been up to for the past few years. I talked about other possibilities available to me after I completed graduate school and through my job. The doctors were very affirming of the choices I had instinctively made in Omaha. It was good to stop and notice, and have someone else notice, what I had accomplished. I swallowed my pride, took responsibility for my errors, and explained what I had learned from them. We talked for six months about whether I had the strength to go through the training all over again.

The psychiatrists gave me a positive report about my readiness for military life. I took it right down to that recruiter, bursting with pride and confidence, and said, "I am ready to reenter the Army."

He went through my papers and agreed, "We can get you in, I think you will get the waiver."

I had about a minute to enjoy the news I had spent two years hoping for before the sergeant threw me a curveball.

"You've been out for long enough now, you know, I think you're going to have to do everything again," he said.

"What?" I wasn't sure I had heard him correctly.

I had heard of people having to do basic or other kinds of training more than once. Normally that's because they're transferring from another branch, or are being recycled because they didn't pass the first time. You also have to repeat training if you have been out of the military for a longer period of time, maybe three years or more. I had passed everything and had been out for less than two years. That couldn't be right. We agreed that he was going to apply for my waiver and check on the training.

While I waited on the waiver and considered the possibility that I would have to return to the Army as a brand-new recruit, I finished graduate school and continued to work.

I was working for myself now. After examining the assessments of independent insurance adjusters and contractors through my work at Mutual of Omaha, I saw that I could make more money and have more flexibility over my hours if I went out on my own. It was the summer of 1999 and there had been some big hurricanes, so I was busy. I had a lot of work that summer and fall, traveling to Miami, Baltimore, and Philadelphia after their storms. I remember going for runs in all these different places and turning my options over in my mind, thinking about whether I was really up for starting from scratch. Around November, I got the call to come back to Omaha and they confirmed that I would have to start from basic training. I decided that I had come too far to quit now and reported for duty.

* * *

When I had my physical for reentry, the doctors noted some old football injuries in my lower back and said I was not going to be able to be 11 Bravo, which is infantry. That is what I had trained for the first time around in Fort Benning. Determined to stay on a path that would get me to Ranger School, I asked if I could be a 91 Bravo, a combat medic. Combat medics can also become Rangers. I still did not have a contract to go back to Ranger Battalion, but I felt pretty confident that I was going to be able to tie up the loose ends once I got back in. They approved me for 91 Bravo, so I signed up and was assigned to basic training in Fort Jackson, South Carolina. I wasn't thrilled about the change, but it was acceptable. I was excited to be making progress toward my goal, and I had never trained at a coed facility like Fort Jackson. But it was not to be. A few weeks later, just two hours before I was due to ship out, my recruiter walked up to say that Fort Benning was going to become a multijob training base, so that not only infantry but artillery and combat support could train there. I would be sent to Fort Benning after all. That would turn out to be a bit of divine intervention.

The recruiter trusted me to drive myself to the airport in Omaha. Tanya dropped me off at Eppley Airfield in Omaha to catch my flight to Atlanta, where I gathered with other recruits to take a bus to Fort Benning. The other guys were all first-timers and full of nervous energy and chatter. Some of them looked scared. Even though I had only a couple years on most of them, I felt so much older. I told them, "Don't worry, guys, it's gonna suck, but you can handle it." Though I knew, better than anybody else on that bus, how much it was going to suck, I still felt excited. I knew what was coming, and I wanted to be there. And I felt confident: I knew, in my bones, that I was physically ready and that I was going to crush the physical training. The bus rolled toward Columbus, and I fell asleep until we were back at the processing station. Walking onto the base felt like a small victory. I might have been returning as a 91 Bravo, but it was like coming home.

* * *

There was a drill sergeant waiting when we arrived at 30th AG Reception Battalion and got off the bus, just like the first time, yet it was different. I'm not sure if the Army was getting a little softer or if I was too experienced, but there was an edgy toughness that had gone missing this time around. The drill sergeant asked if there were prior service guys in the group, and it turned out there were four of us. He asked us to sit tight for a few minutes and then sent us to be processed in a separate facility. People were still barking orders, but it was more laid back; there was no standing at attention in front of the chow hall for what felt like hours.

They assigned the four of us with prior service to an open bay, full of cots with little trunks and lockboxes at the foot of the beds. It looked pretty much like what you might see in a movie, like *Stripes* or *Full Metal Jacket*. As we unpacked, I realized that my experience was giving me an advantage. You can't control every situation, but you can prepare yourself logistically, mentally, and physically for what you're walking into, and I was straight-up better prepared the second time around. I had overpacked during my first rotation in basic and brought things I didn't know I wouldn't be allowed to keep, such as my own Tylenol. I knew not to bring cotton socks, because cotton will tear your feet up. You need wool. I didn't have to wear my old boots. I didn't know the first time that there would be a PX on the base where we could buy basics when we needed them, but there was. This time I knew it, so I had packed a lot lighter. I was oriented, calmer, and better prepared, which is half the battle.

I shined my jungle boots, which I was allowed to wear being prior service, got all my new gear ready, and picked up my issue. We got better clothing compared to my first go-round. I was starting the course in the winter, so the warmer-gear battle dress uniforms (BDUs) might have just been more substantial, but I remember feeling that everything seemed like slightly better quality. I was not allowed to wear my old unit patches on my new uniforms, but I was allowed to keep my Airborne wings, and I got to keep my rank. I had not been in the Ranger Battalion long enough to run a course to earn my Expert Infantryman Badge, which I had wanted to earn. I also hadn't gotten my Ranger tab yet. I was an E-4 specialist without a tab.

They gave us our schedules for classes, PT, and chow, and the drill sergeant asked me to show people around since I had been at Benning before. It was nice not being treated like a private or a newbie. We had the same workload and had to pass the same tests, but the leaders were treating the few of us experienced recruits more like adults. For example, they often let us be responsible for our own PT. That can backfire. Some of the guys who were experienced like me were not in the same kind of shape I was and took advantage of the opportunity to slack. But I generally showed up for PT with the other privates in the morning and always did extra training on my own. Sometimes I ran on Sand Hill in the mornings, doing a five-mile loop before chow. I loved running there on my own on the country road, watching the sun rise in the beautiful Georgia sky. I would listen to the birds calling and hear the sounds of reveille, of the newbies rising and their cadence calls, and then the echo of drill sergeants yelling. I was so conscious of breathing in the clean smell of the red clay dirt that I still think of it as the Benning smell. It takes me back to a place that, in many ways, was painful and exhausting, but it makes me smile because I think of those as some of the best times of my life. At Benning I could feel myself learning, changing, and getting stronger every day.

* * *

The senior drill sergeant called me into his office, and I rushed to report. He had my records in front of him, spread across his desk.

"Specialist Paronto reporting,"

"You were at Regiment before?"

"Yes, Sergeant."

"You were a Batt Boy?"

"Yes sir, Second Battalion, Seventy-fifth."

He looked at me for a long minute before asking "What the fuck are you doing in 91 Bravo? Why are you going to be a medic?"

I explained that I had not made the decision and that I had not received a "picket fence" on my physical. That was how we referred to the physical form to enter basic. The doctors would evaluate various aspects of your body and health and give each a number, like 1 or 2. You want all ones, because that means you have no physical restrictions. When your whole report is a row of ones, we would call that a picket fence.

So I pointed out that the doctors in Omaha had given me a 2 on my back. I told him that it had surprised me because it was an old injury that didn't bother me, but I couldn't argue with it and that 91 Bravo was the best way I knew how to stay on the Ranger path. He shook his head and said, "Motherfucker. They gave you a two. But you want your blue cord back, don't you?"

He was referring to an honorable infantry designation, which I would lose with this switch to being a medic. I affirmed that of course I wanted it back.

"The head doc at the Troop Medical Clinic can take another look at you," he decided, "and then you can go back to infantry and finish what you fucking started." He was a special forces Vietnam combat guy who was now a colonel and for me was an unlikely guardian angel. I retook the test, they made me a picket fence, and, just like that, I got to be 11 Bravo again. I was elated.

After about a week at 30th AG, basic training officially started and I loaded up with the newbies and headed to 1st Battalion, 50th Infantry Basic Training Company, still at Fort Benning. It still sucked, and we were still being smoked as a unit, still riding on the back of cattle cars, towed by a semi. If that isn't demeaning, I don't know what is. But it continued to feel a little softer the second time around. There was yelling, but there wasn't as much of it. There were smoke sessions, but they did not seem as aggressive or intense. I noticed that most of the drill sergeants this time around did not have their Ranger tabs. Either way, I was ready for anything they were going to dish out.

WISDOM FROM THE RANGERS
PRINCIPLE SIX: ACCEPT RESPONSIBILITY; NO EXCUSES

My first couple years in Omaha were not the most dramatic period in my life when you compare them with a firefight in Benghazi. Yet in some ways they were among the most pivotal years of my life. They allowed me to apply the never-quit mind-set to my personal life and see just how determined I could be. Those years helped me understand that success is not about being perfect.

Pride is a deadly sin. You must be able to put pride aside and recognize when you have made mistakes. Take responsibility when you have not been strong. I see a lot of people who seem unwilling or unable to do this, especially politicians in Washington. I see unwillingness to admit mistakes in the media as well, on both sides of the political spectrum. The inability to admit you are fallible is a great weakness and a kind of arrogance. It is also a sin against God, which matters to me.

Being responsible does not mean being perfect. It does mean that you correct your mistakes when you make them. Many people behave badly after making a mistake, com-

pounding the consequences of their bad decisions. When you can be honest with yourself
and take responsibility, you can learn from your
mistakes. You can move on, and you can get
better and stronger if you do so. You need to
slow down and figure out your next productive move.

When you fail or give up a goal, you
lose some self-esteem. You give up some
confidence. You always have options when you
fail. You can choose not to recover. Or you can
accept the failure, figure out a new goal, and
work your ass off going after it. I don't care
how shaken you are in your sense of yourself
or how dramatically you think you have failed.
You can drive on.

Identify the problem, and consider the
possible solutions. Make a plan to accomplish
the solution. Now you're in it. You need to
set another goal. But it all starts with taking
responsibility for your mistakes.

No excuses. If you give yourself this bottom
line throughout your life, you will notice how
often you are tempted to let yourself off the
hook. Do not waste time overanalyzing failure.
Take responsibility, keep making decisions,
take action, and try to stay focused on your
next move. In order to accomplish your mission,

you will need to continue to take action, even when the circumstances are changing and the outcome is uncertain. Sometimes your time frame is urgent, but more often in civilian life, things become urgent because you failed to take action earlier.

Being decisive and taking action is hard for a lot of people, but it's a skill, not just a personality trait, and it is worth getting better at it. I'm not saying that you should make snap decisions, more that you want to be able to make a decision and act on it. Sometimes you might get from point A to point B in an inefficient zigzag pattern, but if you don't take action you won't get to where you need to be at all. If you do your recon, you'll eventually learn to trust your judgment and your rapid decisions will more likely be good ones.

I don't care what kind of mess you have made of your life; as long as you face up to it and try to improve yourself, you still have a chance. You don't know what is going to pan out, either. Not everything you try will work. You will learn from experience. It's easy to remain stagnant, but you will never succeed if you stay passive. You learn by asking questions and by trying things out. My move to Omaha turned out to be a critical decision.

Sometimes you have to take a chance and remove yourself from a negative situation or just get out of the comfort zone, whatever or wherever it is.

If you are prone to self-pity, thinking too much will be your enemy. Being thoughtful is productive, and having feelings is human. But when you are on your own, specifically when you have nothing to do, it's easy to start playing mind games with yourself. Unfortunately, the things that many of us do when we start playing crazy mind games with ourselves make everything worse. When we drink, do drugs, or veg out in front of the TV for too many hours, we avoid our negative feelings, but we also avoid taking productive action to move forward. Most people need an external structure to order their time and find that routines help them stay organized and upbeat. When you have no task that immediately requires your attention and no goal upon which to focus your psychic energy, it's easy to start worrying about whatever problems preoccupy you. That is unproductive. You want to have the discipline to use your alone time to do things that you enjoy and that serve your goals. If you can't do that, have the discipline to impose some kind of structure for yourself to keep from wasting too much time or compounding your problems.

Give yourself some credit, too, for taking care of yourself. I became very independent in Omaha. I didn't ask my parents for help. I paid my own bills and lived within my very meager means. As I learned new skills, eventually I was able to pay the bills on a better apartment and a car and have a little spending money. That is a good feeling. You get a deep sense of satisfaction when you do not use the safety net of your family, the government, or anybody else. I hate that term *safety net*. Do you know what your best safety net is? It is working your ass off, getting a job, and continuing to work your ass off.

We all make mistakes. We all make poor choices. Sometimes we disappoint people we care about or who are counting on us. I struggled after I quit Ranger Battalion because I knew I had disappointed my family. My dad always told me that it's important to finish what you start. When I was a boy, my mom used to tell me how important it is to pick yourself back up when you fall. She also used to invoke her hardworking father, an immigrant who believed that it rests on each of us to succeed, not on anybody else. Their values, and their unwavering belief in me, helped me recover from my mistakes. Do not let your mistakes or misery define you. Commit to owning errors when you make them, learning from your mistakes, and acting with integrity. If you can utilize your bad decisions and hard times as learning experiences, they will make you stronger. You hear that all the time, but it is the truth. Be humble, be patient, be stoic, and be adaptable. If you can learn from your mistakes, you will find that you are better than your worst moment.

Chapter Nine

LEAD

"Rangers, lead the way."
—DIVISION COMMANDER OF THE 29TH INFANTRY DIVISION
DURING THE D-DAY LANDINGS ON OMAHA BEACH, NORMANDY,
FRANCE, TO LIEUTENANT COLONEL MAX SCHNEIDER,
COMMANDER OF THE 5TH RANGER BATTALION

I will always keep myself mentally alert, physically strong,
and morally straight and I will shoulder more than my
share of the task whatever it may be, one hundred
percent and then some.
—RANGER CREED

Exercising leadership is easier when you have confidence in your own judgment and competence. Leaders have a clear understanding of their overall mission and the tasks before them. They recognize the strengths and weaknesses of their team and situation, and they utilize those strengths while minimizing the effect of their vulnerabilities. They communicate clearly, including giving orders when they need to. They take orders when they need to and recognize when they need help. Being a leader also means doing the right thing: you don't take the easy wrong over the hard right. In combat, taking the hard right means walking into a situation where you may lose your life. It's a real possibility.

Ranger School is a course that the Army calls "the most physically and mentally demanding leadership school [we have] to offer." Graduating from Ranger School is not a prerequisite for serving in a Ranger unit, but it is required in order to have a leadership position and remain in the unit. The training is painful, miserable, and risky. Soldiers have died of heatstroke and hypothermia during Ranger School. Historically, less than half the candidates in any given class complete the program and earn their black-and-gold tab. Everyone who enters Ranger School is willing to step up and be a leader, and the Army gives us an opportunity to prove we can do so. We will be responsible for executing critical missions and for protecting equipment and assets and one another in life-threatening situations. That stuff matters, and the Army doesn't make it easy for people to get the opportunity to try it.

The paths to Ranger School can vary. I completed basic training, Airborne School, and then the Ranger Indoctrination Program (RIP), which is not uncommon (except for my having done basic and RIP twice), but there are alternative avenues to Ranger School. Once I successfully completed RIP, I was assigned to the 75th Ranger Regiment. But completing RIP is not the same as earning your Ranger tab. The tab is a mark of distinction and testament to the ability to lead under the toughest conditions possible. To earn the tab, I had to graduate from Ranger School. The leaders at the 75th Ranger Regiment decide who may go to Ranger School and when they are ready. We all prove our readiness by constantly training for both short-term contingency missions and ongoing combat operations.

HOW READY ARE YOU?

When I was in RIP the second time, I was ready for anything. My intense physical training in Omaha served me well, and I distinguished myself early on by destroying the PT tests. I could do more than a hundred push-ups and sit-ups in the two minutes, get right up and max a two-mile run in under a six-minute pace, then follow up with thirty pull-ups. My PT performance earned me some respect early on, and though the day-to-day was still miserable, it was less so the second time around. There was still hazing, but it didn't seem quite as intense. Some of that was external, because there were no Space Invaders games this time around. I'm not sure if the Army was cracking down on that kind of behavior or if I happened into a group with a different dynamic. Probably both. But some of the difference was due to my own attitude, because we still took plenty of crap. There were still lots of "tab checks!" where anyone without a tab had to drop to the floor and start doing push-ups. There was also lots of what we used to call "koala-fying." That's where we had to run to a tree, grab the trunk, flip upside down, and hold on to it as long as we could. It's tough and awkward and everyone eventually falls headfirst. Imagine fifteen guys doing that at once. But I played the games and didn't let them get to me, I was just determined to move through the training. I knew that I could endure it because I had already done it once and I knew it would end.

Once I finally got back to where I'd been when I was discharged, serving in the 75th Ranger Regiment and hoping to go to Ranger School, I was determined to excel. We did a training exercise that required doing a ruck march several miles out into the range and then doing live fires all day and night fires in the field. Some of the fields were closer to the barracks than others, but I preferred marching further away, because if I have to sleep out on the ground, I'd rather not see civilization nearby and think about a bed.

One night we were shooting, and I was tired. I had become a machine gunner, a leader on a machine-gun team. We had to get up and get down each time we were told to move, and I had been jumping up to move and getting down into a prone position holding an M240 Bravo for about a day and half. Because we were still untabbed, we also had to run and move water and food out in the field between movements, do push-ups, or do basically anything else asked of us. So I was exhausted and looking forward to finishing our rounds, because once we used up our ammunition, we would be done for the night. Like just about everything else, we were on the clock for this exercise, and I did not want our team to come in last.

We got an order to move, and I went to load more ammunition and realized that something was wrong with my machine gun. I couldn't manipulate the carrying handle to pick it up and move to my next firing position. It could have been me just being beat tired, but it seemed as though something was wrong with the carrying handle. We needed to move, and I was determined not to fail this training op. We had been shooting all day, and I could see the barrel glow in my night vision goggles because it was so hot. I knew it was going to hurt, but I reached down with my Nomex gloves, grabbed the buttstock with my right hand, and picked up the base of the barrel with my left hand. Then I ran as fast as I could to my next position and set the gun up on the bipod legs to continue firing. The left-hand glove had started to melt onto the barrel, so I had to use my right hand to pull my left hand off of it. That did the trick, and I was able to pick up my gun and continue shooting.

Now, I really wanted to get the exercise done, so I went cyclic and held the trigger down to get rid of the rest of the rounds as quickly as possible. Going cyclic might have saved us a couple of minutes, but I was risking the machinery, and our leadership noticed. My squad leader had his night vision on and saw how hot my barrel was glowing.

"Paronto, look at your damn barrel! If you don't change your barrel, you're going to shoot it out!"

He smoked us and we deserved it, but, man, was that a tough time for me to have to do push-ups. As my body weight pressed my palms into the ground again and again, I knew I had really done a number on myself.

When we were finally released, I pulled off what was left of my glove and saw a burn across my left hand from the index finger down to my wrist, with a huge blister still forming in front of my eyes. It hurt like hell, but I didn't say a word because I didn't want to disrupt the op. I figured I would power through until I could get back to see a medic in the morning. By the time we marched back at sunrise, I looked as though I had a small balloon on my palm. I asked for permission to see the medic, and when the squad leader asked me why, I showed him my hand. I remember his eyes widened and he looked up at me and demanded, "What the fuck happened?" I explained that I hadn't been able to get my carrying handle in place while we were moving the night before, but I hadn't wanted to lose, so I'd just grabbed the barrel while it was heated and it had melted my glove and burned my skin. There was a long pause before he said, "Hell yeah, go see the doc."

He didn't say anything else. But I could see in his face that I had just proved something to him. I hadn't set out to do it, and maybe it hadn't been the smartest move, but I had just demonstrated toughness. When someone fights through pain, that is someone you can depend on. That is someone who will do what it takes to get the job done. He assigned me to Ranger School shortly afterward.

Of course that story is nothing in comparison to what some others have gone through to get a real job done. Guys fight through serious injuries during actual firefights, or they continue to fight after seeing a buddy injured or killed at their side. That is true grit.

* * *

I was ecstatic to finally be going to Ranger School. It felt like I was making progress toward my professional goals, and I was happy in my personal life, settling into my second marriage. But now I would be gone for three months, and I knew there would be very little contact with the outside world, not even by phone, during that time. It would be my first real separation from my wife, and I was sad about it. I think I was also nervous because I felt that the physical separation had contributed to the failure of my first marriage. So, the anticipation was screwing with me and I didn't sleep the night before I left. But I reminded myself how hard I had worked for this and tried to have faith that everything would work out. It's still hard to leave my family behind on deployments. But I try to think of it as though I'm just going to work. My nine-to-five is just longer than most people's.

Ranger School itself has three phases—Benning Phase, Mountain Phase, Swamp Phase—and each one is designed to give you experience with combat conditions that are specific to their environment. In each phase, we are sleeping outdoors, moving quickly with heavy gear, and learning to perform on little sleep while eating one or two meals each day while we prepare to engage in direct-fire battles and close combat. In addition to learning military mountaineering and how to lead units on combat patrols, airborne, air assault, and small-boat operations, we might practice leading a platoon-sized patrol and how to plan and execute different kinds of combat missions while in a state of extreme physical and mental stress.

* * *

Before we actually began Ranger School, we spent the first three weeks learning infantry tactics in a state of sleep deprivation. This pre-Ranger phase was not unlike RIP. The pre-Ranger barracks are even physically near the RIP barracks. There were land navigation courses that might last all day or all night, and we were never permitted to sleep for more than three or four hours at a time. Those weeks were miserable because I felt that I was starting to get physically beaten down but that it wasn't getting me anywhere because I hadn't yet started the school itself.

We would work on battle drills, small-unit tactics, and going out to ranges in Fort Benning to practice assaulting a bunker or maneuvering on a bunker or a live fire range. Many of the tasks we were assigned were things we had done before, but now we were perfecting those skills as a squad. We did get fed, though I did not appreciate it properly at the time and would think back on it longingly later in the training, when we were training in a constant state of hunger. But it sucked already. My knees hurt from having to crawl everywhere, and guys were getting yelled at constantly because we were all still untabbed. Sometimes I would wonder what I was getting out of it. I was impatient to get started on what I thought of as the "real" phases of Ranger School.

Once we started Ranger School, we were not just training to act, we were also training to lead. Part of perfecting our tactics as a team was learning how to lead and follow one another effectively. We did a final exercise in the pre-

Ranger phase where the whole platoon assaulted a compound. Everyone rotated through various positions during the mission. I was a squad leader at one point and a team leader at another point. In each case we had to figure out how to get guys to do what we need them to do when everyone was tired. Everyone was angry, hurting, beat, and anxious to move on to the next phase. Most people were feeling a little selfish, but we all had a mission to accomplish. As leaders, we are responsible for motivating guys who don't particularly want to be motivated. It's trial and error, and that is as much a part of the learning experience as the actual ground tactics. Guys yell, guys cheer, people stop and start listening, but everyone has to figure out how to keep moving their mission forward.

Certain aspects of Benghazi were better than I'd had it in Ranger School. I faced those thirteen hours in Benghazi on a good night's sleep and a full belly. During training, sometimes guys would fall out from fatigue during those forced marches with the rucksacks. Those of us who could carry a lot of weight would sometimes grab their stuff and carry it for a bit when it seemed as if they were losing it. We needed everyone to keep going. It's not possible to baby people and cover for them all the time, but sometimes it's OK to cut them a break. We learned how to set the example, help people who were flagging to keep going, and show them what was possible: "Look, I'm marching with my ruck and your ruck. It can be done. It's possible. You got this. It is a matter of will."

Ranger School is sometimes described as a tough two-month leadership course, but people don't understand the half of it. The pace felt glacial as I got closer to actually starting. I was relieved and excited to finally move to Camp Darby and begin, but even then, there were two more weeks that tested my patience. Ranger School started with "Zero Week," where we joined other units who became part of our class, followed by "Ranger Assessment Phase (RAP)." RAP Week included another series of physical tests, including the famous Malvesti and Darby Queen obstacle courses. There are many Ranger-inspired fitness programs and courses, and you may be familiar with Malvesti's infamous worm pit, which is a twenty-five-meter, muddy obstacle covered with barbed wire. The Darby Queen course had to be negotiated as part of a buddy team, and my partner was a new "butter bar," a second lieutenant from the Infantry Officer Basic Leader Course, who was out of shape, so I got to do a number of those obstacles over and over alongside him until he could pass. As far as I was concerned, we spent about a month and a half under tremendous stress, getting our bodies torn up, and we hadn't even started yet.

Whether or not we graduated from Ranger School depended on our performance in various leadership positions in various situations, usually twice during each phase. The Ranger instructors (RIs) who were evaluating us would give us a "go" if we met the standards set for the operation or a "no go" if we did not. No one can move on to the next phase without the "go," and no one can have more than one unsuccessful patrol per phase. If you include the three-week pre-Ranger phase of training, as well as Zero Week and RAP Week, I was five weeks in by the time I felt we were really starting to move forward. The stress of the previous weeks was catching up with us when we were doing op orders, which are the planning portion of an operation before you go out to do your patrols. They take place in an outside classroom, which is basically bleachers with wooden shelters and a mobile chalkboard. Even though it was cold and uncomfortable, I would start to fall asleep when we sat still because I was so worn out. We were so tired that some of us would put chewing tobacco in the corners of our eyes to try to irritate them and keep us awake.

Because sleep and food are pretty low priorities in combat, Ranger School was designed to give us a sense of what it feels like and how to deal with it. The past few weeks were catching up with us. When we were staying at the barracks, we were forced to eat extremely quickly, literally in less than five minutes. There was no talking allowed, but no one would bother because we had so little time. We could use only a spoon. As winter Rangers, we were given two MREs (meals ready to eat) for each day we were out in the field and we could eat them whenever we wanted to. They were allegedly giving us 2,200 calories each day, but we were easily expending three times that amount of energy. Some guys would get so hungry they would eat all their MREs during a single chow time and then starve for a few days, depending on the op and the resupply. Learning to ration those meals properly was a lesson in discipline and patience. Summer Rangers generally just get one MRE meal a day. So I guess I should have counted my blessings. But I was not in a grateful mood: I had not been getting enough calories, certainly not for the past two or two and a half weeks, and I was starting to feel that during everyday activities. Six-mile runs that should have been easy were starting to feel slow.

I got picked to be squad leader for a mission during a three-day op. Infantry platoons are usually made up of three rifle squads and a weapons squad. This was a relatively early training op, so we were graded as squad and team leaders and an RI acted as the platoon leader. The op was a raid on a pretend satellite facility. There was going to be an air assault mission, so we were going to be riding in UH-60 Black Hawk helicopters and we had to do a load plan. We would be flying in on those, jumping down, and then have to move. Leadership assignments can rotate within a mission, and I was assigned to be Alpha team leader, essentially the point man of the movement, so my job was to get us to our objective. I was commanding my fire team, which consisted of a rifleman, an automatic gunner, a grenadier, and a scout rifleman.

We flew to our helicopter landing zone in the Black Hawks. As the point guy, I was at the edge of the door. It doesn't matter how long I've been doing this, I still love flying on those. I remember flying in along the tree line that day and thinking how cool it was to see the leaves beginning to turn colors from up there. Even though it was autumn, it was still pretty green in Georgia. But there wasn't much time for reflection or admiring the foliage. The helos touched down briefly in a clearing in the woods and we did a straight jump out, with no rappelling or fast roping, and then the helos took off. It felt surreal because it was so quick. I love to watch the helos bank and fly away, but there was no time to look that day. We hit the ground, and people were spread out everywhere; this was a whole platoon's worth of guys, jumping out of four helicopters. The first thing I needed to do was consolidate my guys, get a count, and have us form a 360-degree cover and concealment as though we were in enemy territory. I knew my direction, my map, my route plan, and my objective: we were meant to maneuver around an enemy camp and sneak in, complete the mission, and sneak out without any altercations.

Remember, we were all rookies. We were all still learning, and everyone was beat down and hungry from the last three weeks. Once we established 360-degree security, the leadership came together in the middle and did a quick map check. I needed to look at the terrain to figure out if we had landed where we were supposed to. We were not allowed to use GPS, so we were reading our little military maps and using our compasses to establish our location. We pointed at the map with our fingers as we conferred and then began to move toward the objective, which was based off my step count from our planned location. We got into formation and started moving, spreading out in wedge formations by squad, as planned. There was a road we were going to use as our backstop as we headed north to the objective, and sure enough, we found a road. But I got a funny feeling in the pit of my stomach. We shouldn't have hit that road yet. Something was off. I told the squad leader, and we examined the terrain and looked at the map again. We thought maybe it should be the road, but I wasn't sure. I didn't trust myself. The RI acting as platoon leader was accompanying us to observe, and he started putting the pressure on us to make a decision: "Hurry up, Ranger! Are you going to get your troops in order or what?" He would be evaluating our performance. I had to make the call. Another platoon was doing the same op, and I thought I could hear them, which also made me nervous. We didn't want to link up with another platoon in that situation, because then we could all become a huge target. I decided to trust my pace count and keep moving forward.

When we got to where the road should have been, it wasn't there. My stomach just dropped. I knew I had screwed up, but I wasn't sure how. Then we started to hear sounds of an engagement. There was a firefight going on, and I wondered if that meant another platoon had stumbled into the enemy camp. Their chaotic noise added to my sense of dread about being in the wrong spot. Again, everyone was looking at me to make the call about how to proceed.

I could have reversed course and let our fourth unit lead us back until we got our bearings, but I decided to reorient and shoot up north. That was correct, and to my relief, we regained our location. We set up another objective rally point so the leadership could conduct a recon and map check. That meant that the platoon created a circle and provided security while the team leaders conferred and reconned the objective. We revised and made our quick plan: we got our distances, what direction we were coming in from, and who was supporting whom. Finally, we executed. We hit our objective, but it wasn't flawless, by any means. It was our first time working together as a team, and it was ragged. We did not have good control. Guys were going out in front of one another's muzzles, getting in one another's line of fire: in the end it was successful, but it was a rookie mess.

Once we had cleared the objective, we gathered for a scheduled change of leadership. Someone else would be in charge for the next phase, to get us out of the objective and back to the patrol base. I was scheduled to be a grenadier for that part of the mission. They don't tell you right in the field that you passed or failed, but I knew. We might have cleared the objective, but I was going to get a "no go" for the operation. We made our leadership change and got ready to head for the patrol base, where we would rest for the night. It was getting dark. I switched weapons with the grenadier, put on my night vision goggles, and started moving. Between the Kevlar helmet and the old-school Cyclops-style night vision goggles I had on, my head felt about as heavy as my heart. As it turned out, I had a lot of time to think about everything that had just happened, because things did not go smoothly for the leaders of that phase either. We walked and walked and walked because they had trouble reading the map, and it took us close to six hours to walk four kilometers while they tried to figure out where we were. It would have been funnier if we hadn't been marching up and down the same mountain during parts of it and if we hadn't all been tripping over the climbing "catch me" vines that cover the Georgia woods in the dark. We finally reached the area the RIs had designated to set up our patrol base at one in the morning.

I knew that even though we had gotten our objective, I was going to get chewed out, and I was right. The RIs who had been observing us went through the list of what we had done right and the very long list of what we had done wrong. Two major mistakes stood out.

My original mistake came when I had read my map after we did the jump. We had landed in the proper spot. But I had used my finger when I was pointing out our location on the map. You never point at a map with your finger in that situation. The map is tiny, and a finger is too damn big. I should have used something like a pine needle. The objective was based off my step count from the location, and my original location was off by about 500 meters because I had pointed to the map with the tip of my finger. Because our distance and direction were based on the pace count, even though my pace count was correct, we went well past our checkpoints. That was a stupid mistake, and you can bet I've never made it again.

But I did something even worse. Another platoon was in a firefight, and we did not offer to provide help. Of course we should have helped! The other platoon was getting hammered, and we did not offer any support. Boy, did the RI rip into us over that: "What is wrong with you? Are you going to let your buddies go to war and not support them? How many people would have died because you didn't provide assistance?" He was absolutely right. I was so concerned about my own performance, getting my "go," that I lost sight of the larger objectives and prioritized myself over others.

I have thought a lot about that bad choice since then. Sometimes we can become so focused on our own situations, we don't even see when someone else needs us. I have seen many people who are more worried about making rank or appeasing the person above them than in helping a buddy or doing the right thing. Leaders know that helping a buddy or family member is always the right thing, even if it makes us look bad on an evaluation or pisses someone off. To me, in a larger sense, that happened in Benghazi. The CIA, the State Department, the Department of Defense: we are all part of a team fighting against terrorism. As far as I'm concerned, some people put their careers ahead of helping our team that night.

As a leader, you never want to ask anyone to do something that you haven't already done or that you aren't willing to do yourself. That was part of the leadership failure of Benghazi. I don't think our leaders had ever seen anything like that and they didn't seem willing to go out front and move toward that gunfire. The first thirty minutes of an attack situation is essential if you are going to keep any kind of advantage. As time goes by, you continually lose any advantage you might have because the attack continues whether you're there or not.

* * *

The military teaches us to respect our leaders, which does not always go hand in hand with liking them. Someone can lead in a way that teaches us something, and he or she can earn respect, if not affection, and that is one thing. We can't control who is put in charge. We can respect that they have earned the right to command us, by going through the same training and actually serving in the situations we have trained for, and we obey their commands. But just because someone is a leader in title doesn't make him or her a good leader. That turned out to be true in Benghazi. Our chief of base, Bob, and our team leader locked up in a moment of crisis. I feel they did not use the assets they had available, which at that moment included two Navy SEALs, three Marines, and an Army Ranger. Our team stepped into what we considered a leadership void.

Bottom-up leadership occurs when a situation demands that someone take charge. Our team was clear about our mission and our values: Americans were under attack, and we were supposed to help them. We knew when it was time to challenge our leadership and break the rules because we had confidence in our judgment. Luckily, in Benghazi, our entire team was full of leaders. The GRS team was trained to react and understood what was necessary to move forward. We also knew how to listen and trust one another and how to communicate.

We were continually talking to one another and keeping track of one another, even when we were split up. We also put differences aside. No one tried to take control, and no one needed to tell anyone else what to do. We all had different specialties and skill sets, and we relied on one another's expertise. Good leaders recognize when other people can be responsible. Boon was our best sniper, and he had the sniper rifle. We didn't discuss it or argue about it, and there was no reason to give it to anybody else. We wanted to utilize people's strengths, so he belonged in the best fighting position. I don't have a problem running toward gunfire. I'm not saying I'm fearless—maybe I'm just stupid—but when we started getting hit at the consulate, I was the first person firing back, even though I was out in the open. Rone was an angel, our defacto leader, and our rock. Jack pays incredible attention to detail and was probably the most meticulous of our team, so he was the one keeping tabs on the interpreter and always making sure our security was in place. Tig would give his life for anybody, which is a huge strength, enabling him to run and fight fearlessly. Oz is unbelievably tough, which was clear to anyone who worked with him long before they saw him continue to fight with his arm almost blown off. It was almost instinctive that night, the way everyone was able to fall out and utilize his unique assets.

Experience matters. Our experiences, our mistakes, and what we had learned from them informed our leadership. Everyone defending the Annex in Benghazi on September 11 was a veteran soldier or Marine with leadership experience, and it showed. We had all been noncommissioned officers or commissioned officers in our respective services. While we were waiting for the "go" order in Benghazi, we were listening to the sounds of the battle on the radio and trying to analyze the conditions out there. When we responded in a moment of crisis, we were going back and pulling from all our experiences. We were also thinking about what we needed in that situation and trying to make decisions. Air support? Let's make some calls to get that in. Weapons systems? Let's get those in order so that we're good to go. Check it, is everything working properly? Do we have the right ammunition? Radio communication: Are we all on the right levels? Are our vehicles working properly? What's the plan? When we drive out of here, which route are we going to take? Because we had five experienced guys in a state of readiness, we were able to answer those questions and be ready in minutes.

I thought about former leaders, previous simulations, and my old drill sergeants and how they had kept their composure. When we were under heavy fire, I flashed on past leaders talking about Rangers jumping into Panama in 1989 under heavy fire with no cover and shooting their way through. They didn't go high or try to take cover, they just started shooting. I thought about that at the consulate. And we went toward the fire, because that's what my leaders had done and what we had been trained to do. I pulled from those memories and experiences, and they helped me stay composed.

Leaders never give up hope. Keeping adrenaline and stress levels in check is an important part of being a good leader. When we were back at the base in Benghazi in between firefights on September 11, I went looking for another pair of night vision goggles because mine had broken. I found our chief of base, Bob, sitting in the middle of the room, on the floor. He was leaning back against the wall with his head in his hands and his elbows on his knees. That is the posture of defeat. Maybe he didn't feel defeated, I don't know. But I saw it, and so did others. It pissed me off. When you are a leader, people are watching you, and, like it or not, they will feed off your attitude and posture. It might have been a devastating night for him, but he did not show leadership in that pose. I gave him a cell phone I'd found at the consulate and said, "Hey, I think this might belong to the ambassador." I wanted to be positive. I wanted to say, "Hey, we're still in this, we've got this, let's keep moving." That is from Ranger School. We were taught to expect success and to pass that belief on to the people we were leading.

WISDOM FROM THE RANGERS

PRINCIPLE SEVEN: LEADERS TAKE THE HARD RIGHT, NEVER THE EASY WRONG

Leadership comes from being responsible for other people, setting an example, and making tough calls under stressful circumstances. We start to develop the ability to do that in Ranger training when we are assigned to lead a unit. In the military, the first step is not really learning how to do something that is technically correct but about learning how to be nervous and not turn away. Yes, you are going to screw up; yes, you might fail; yes, it could be dangerous; yes, it's going to hurt. You learn to walk toward the bad stuff, even though you know it's going to suck. SEALS, Rangers, and Marines learn that.

They are trained to take charge in austere environments and genuinely miserable conditions. The only thing that is simulated is that you are not actually being shot at with real bullets. Otherwise, you are leading other guys who are truly hungry, cold, tired, and hurting. You are graded on how effectively you can motivate those guys under such conditions. And you need to be humble enough to ask for help when you need it, when you know you're dragging or someone else's knowledge or skill is an asset. Setting aside your own pride and trusting your team are a form of leadership.

You don't need to harm yourself to prove that you are willing to go the extra mile. But you can be conscious about whether or not your attitude and behavior demonstrate your commitment to achieving your goals. Whether you think you're done or not, you have to stay positive. Even if you feel as if you're faking it, you don't give up. You want people to keep moving, even if you have to drag them by their shirt collars. The minute you give up, you'll lose. Especially in combat. If you give up in a firefight, you're dead. In civilian life, when you admit defeat, it might be different, but when you give up, you've lost. Maybe you give up on a big project that you wanted. Might as well let your competitor win it.

Leadership is helping people understand that success really is a matter of will. Sometimes all you can do in a given situation is plod through and keep going. There are rarely magic solutions to make things easier. Accept that things are not going to get any easier, suck up the negative if there is no other way to do it, and keep climbing that mountain to get to your objective. In Benghazi, we were doing everything we could with everything we had. We couldn't change our resources. We couldn't conjure up a radio with direct access to air support or a supporting Ranger battalion, or we would have. We requested everything we wanted and needed, but we were not the decision makers. Sometimes you need to accept the limits of your assets and resources and make the best of what you've got.

There will be times when it is miserable to be a leader. In the military, people may die under your watch. You have to accept that. You need to take your responsibility seriously and act with integrity. When leaders make decisions that take factors into account that aren't about saving people's lives or winning a battle, such as protecting people's names or the mission we were on in Benghazi, which is still classified, their decision-making process is muddied and they are less effective. An example on the civilian side might be a leader who is charged with protecting the reputation of a company. If the company you are protecting is doing something illegal, say, poisoning the water, then continuing to protect it is not leadership. Then you're just being a yes-man. Good leaders do the right thing when no one else is looking, even if it may cost them something personally. That is integrity. If the leaders of a company fail to disclose that they are making an unsafe or defective product because they don't want to endanger their jobs, that is the easy wrong. That is also greed. That demands bottom-up leadership, even if you think it could adversely affect your career. Leaders set a standard and expect others to meet it. Leaders do what they need to do without looking for recognition or being asked to do it.

Learning to lead as a Ranger is grueling because the work we do can have life-or-death consequences. The confidence you learn from being able to execute on those responsibilities is real and stays with you. But you will not execute immediately. You will screw up. It seems as though everything about Ranger School is designed to make you fail, and some of it is. Leaders learn from failure. My failures in Ranger School helped me to act and lead in Benghazi.

What is the relevance of this kind of training to a civilian? I'm not telling you about all this misery so you can experience a sense of schadenfreude or even so you can have a moment to appreciate how easy you have it. It's not that I think everyone has to be a Ranger, or should be combat ready, in order to lead. But very few of us really put ourselves into a situation in which we will truly be tested, pushed to our physical and mental limits, and discover the confidence and pride that comes from surmounting genuine obstacles. That makes a leader. To achieve your full potential and be of service to others, you need to truly know yourself by having been tested.

Chapter Ten

BE CONFIDENT

Gallantly will I show the world that I am a specially selected and well-trained Soldier. My courtesy to superior officers, neatness of dress, and care of equipment shall set the example for others to follow.
—RANGER CREED

Fear is powerful. We waste time when we try to avoid fear, because it is a universal human emotion and every last one of us will experience it. It is better to learn how to recognize and understand fear when we feel it and figure out how to make it a friend. The adrenaline rush we get from fear is a survival instinct. Fear can be a warning that something is wrong. It can be an accurate acknowledgment of a risky situation, and it can become a paralyzing obstacle if it is not properly managed. When I am confident, I can assess any fear and respond to it appropriately. With confidence, fear can even be used like a kind of fuel.

* * *

When I first flew into Baghdad as a contractor with Blackwater in 2004, I was nervous. Scott Helvenston, a former Navy SEAL working with Blackwater, had been killed with his team in the Fallujah ambush of March 2004, just a few months earlier. Their team of four had been transporting equipment and food to Fallujah in unarmored vehicles when they were attacked and killed by insurgents. Their bodies were beaten and burned, and two of their corpses were hung from a bridge. The images and circumstances of their deaths, which had been widely publicized, were heavy on my mind. The Blackwater trainers had made it clear that violence was a real possibility and that, as contractors, we would not have full military support. So I was tense as we approached Baghdad in a little Casa prop airplane from Jordan. We flew in making evasive maneuvers so that no one could get a lock on us, spinning in little circles on a steep descent.

We landed at the international airport, and the Blackwater guys who were already there were waiting to link up with us on the other side of customs. We were going to drive down a road nicknamed "Route Irish" from the airport to the city of Baghdad, it was the most dangerous route there at that time. It was targeted and hit constantly by the enemy because it was used to transport supplies by US military convoys and contractors. Camp Victory, which was one of the biggest Army bases in Iraq at the time, was also off that route.

The Blackwater guys gave us rifles, which were not zeroed to my particular eyesight, but they were something. I had been trained to be able to adjust when my laser was off, and I knew how to fix it on the fly. We can't call time out to fix our sights either in combat or in training. My new colleagues gave me a plate carrier with body armor and M4 magazines. My body was coursing with adrenaline. I had no idea what was going to happen, and waiting to find out, as always, was the worst.

Guys had just died there. I had watched the videos from Fallujah of the bodies being dragged through the streets. Blackwater had also showed us footage of carnage and destroyed vehicles from other sites as a learning experience, to show us what was possible. All those images were in my mind. That is where anticipation sucks. I started playing mind games with myself, wondering what could happen and creating worst-case scenarios. I'd had weeks to think it all over before landing in Baghdad, and now that I was actually there, my mind was starting to play tricks on me. I was starting to have negative, nervous thoughts: "Holy shit, how long am I going to be here? Oh man, will I ever see my family again? Will I get shot?" I had never been gone from my family for so many months before, and that had also started weighing on me.

I couldn't get the magazine into my M4 because I was so nervous. I wrestled with it for a minute and then actually dropped the magazine on the ground. When a magazine hits the ground, especially when that ground is made of concrete, it makes a distinct sound, kind of a hollow metallic slap, and everyone turned and looked at me. The head Blackwater guy was clearly having second thoughts about me, and who could blame him? He asked me what unit I had been with, and I told him I was a Ranger. He didn't say it, but I could tell he was thinking, "This guy was a Ranger? This one, who can't get his M4 loaded?" It was a hell of a first impression.

After I got my weapon loaded, we walked to the cars and I was just hoping we wouldn't get shot. Most people got into Suburbans but I got into a truck with one other guy. It was unarmored, so we rolled the windows down and hung body armor out the windows over the sides of the vehicle for some makeshift protection. I took a deep breath and reminded myself that that was what I had come here to do. I told myself, "You're nervous, big deal. You've been nervous before. Shit is going to happen. You can deal with it. Rely on your training. Be confident. You can handle any situation." As we started to drive, I felt myself calm down. Once I started rolling and doing my job, all the negative nervousness disappeared. I was being active.

As I got oriented, I could focus on the specific moment, and I was able to see it clearly. It was my first time in the Middle East, so I was taking in the beauty of the blue sky and some of the architecture. I looked at the roofs and the burned-out cars on the side of the road, the detritus of war. I might have been on Route Irish in a soft-skinned vehicle with armor hanging out the windows, but I felt strangely lucky. I thought, Who gets to come to Baghdad, Iraq, right now, in the middle of all the shit that is going on? It was a turning point for me, a sense of rightness about putting my training into action. That was where I needed to be. Once I got moving, things felt fine. Anticipation made me productive as I started to use its energy instead of letting it use me.

DON'T PANIC

What would have happened if everything had not gone well when we started moving? Leaders know that they will be surprised. They expect it. Rangers go through extensive planning before any mission, but no mission goes exactly the way we plan it. Ever. When we are off plan, we draw from our experiences, our instincts, and our ability to control our emotions. We learn to accept, and even embrace, adrenaline and nervousness when we feel them and work to turn those feelings into positive energy. We are taught that if we keep moving forward, others will follow. We are also taught to solve each problem one at a time.

I wasn't able to zero the infrared laser of my weapon accurately during one of our firefights at the Annex in Benghazi. Because my laser was not accurately zeroed, my first shot actually landed ten feet left of the guy I was trying to hit. I did not panic. I had been through it before, and I knew what to do. I obviously did not have time to zero my weapon at that moment, so I did what we call "Kentucky windage": I moved my laser over ten feet and just started shooting ten feet to the right of the targets, adjusting as the distance of my targets increased or decreased. It worked. My laser was screwed up, but I figured out another way to do what I needed to. That kind of problem solving is the result of a combination of preparation, decision making, confidence, and staying calm.

* * *

Many of our training exercises at RIP give us the opportunity to practice staying calm and confident in the face of fear. For example, we had to pass three water confidence tests. The first one required each of us to jump blindfolded into a pool from twenty feet high and swim to the side while holding on to our gun. We lost some guys doing that, because some people panic if they swallow water with that blindfold on and the instructors recycle people who don't pass the test. The second test required us to jump off a diving board into a pool with our weapon, in full gear, including our load-carrying equipment (LCE). In that test, we had to unstrap our LCE and find our way to the side of the pool while maintaining control of the weapon. It's honestly pretty easy, as long as you don't panic in the water. The final test had us thrown into the pool in full gear and required us to swim twenty meters or so with our weapons while weighted down by our heavy LCE and boots. To me, those tests were less about a swimming skill or combat task and more about staying focused under duress. Water confidence tests are repeated in RIP, pre-Ranger, and Ranger School, so you practice the skills and experience the stress over and over.

Ranger training is full of learning opportunities that not only are about perfecting a skill but are also meant to give you the chance to perform, or not, under tremendous stress. Land navigation is new to most people in RIP training, so everyone has to learn that skill. We were given a map, a compass, and a protractor and taught how to find grid coordinates, both on paper and in the field. Poles with numbered cubes were spread across about a hundred acres of Cole Range, and we were sent out to find particular points from our grid coordinates. The clock was ticking as we did that, and the time frames we were given to finish them in got shorter as we went along. At first, we did it together as a squad, then as a buddy team, and then, eventually, alone. We might do it once in the morning, once in the afternoon, and once at night. Nights were harder, of course, and we were not allowed to use a regular flashlight. We could use little L-shaped periscope-style lights with a red filter, as you may have seen in old movies. They were the same lights soldiers used in the Vietnam War era, and they protected us from being seen but didn't give us much light to illuminate the way.

A lot of people are spooked by doing night navigation on their own. Being alone at night the first time is tough: we're sent into the pitch dark with no flashlight, and coyotes are howling. I kept slipping and getting slapped by branches. Some of the grid coordinates were near a pond that had alligators in it, so I had to worry about slipping near that, too. I remember getting spooked by a snake slithering by my feet. It stopped me dead in my tracks before we both continued on our separate ways. I could feel my heart racing and I started to panic a bit in the silence. Noise travels in the field, especially at night, and when I had done previous exercises, sometimes I could hear other guys finding different points, but I didn't hear anyone else during my first night out on my own. I wondered if I was lost. My stomach tightened as I began to doubt my measurements, my equipment, and myself. It was a training exercise and I did have a whistle that I could blow if I really got lost, but I didn't want to use it.

My experience of panic is a feeling as though my brain is getting stopped up and everything gets smaller. I focus on the wrong things and begin to cycle through all the possible things that could still go wrong. That kind of thinking is paralyzing. I started thinking about the snake and the coyotes and the silence, and for a moment I just stopped. I stood there, lost in the dark, and didn't know what to do. But I took a deep breath and thought about what the RIP cadre had taught us: when you get lost, find a point or landmark that you know, go to it, find it on your map, and then go shoot an azimuth. An azimuth is an angle measurement between points that we measure with a compass. Over the past four days, I had gotten to know the landscape a bit. I decided to walk north until I found a dirt road I remembered, and then I found the intersection on the map and reshot my azimuth. Once I got my bearings, I was annoyed with myself and began worrying that I wasn't going to be able to get my points in on time. I started running, slipping on the dark trails and getting scratched up. Miraculously, and just barely, I made my time. The sergeant in charge knew how close I had cut it, and I remember him looking at me as I handed him my points, still breathing heavy, and he said, "You're fucking lucky, aren't you, Ranger?" I answered the only way I could: "Roger that, Sergeant."

Other guys were not so lucky that night. We were all still learning, and some of them did get lost. Unfortunately, the rest of us needed to stand at attention until the last man came in. I believe I got in around 11 p.m. and it was after 1 a.m. when everyone was in. It doesn't sound like much after everything else we had been through, but if you try to stand at attention for two hours, you can experience a semblance of that feeling. It is true misery. Yet there was also humor: some of the guys were so tired that they would fall asleep standing up and trip over their own rucks before righting themselves, and we would all laugh for a second before snapping back to attention. I can still call up the physical memory of that feeling of misery in my muscles, and I was still concerned that some of my points were wrong. But I also remember looking at the stars, hearing the coyotes, laughing at my buddies, and feeling peaceful. I felt I had accomplished something. I had a little taste of the satisfaction and confidence that can come from overcoming fear and solving your own problem. I know I carried that sense of competence into Benghazi.

* * *

Our delay in Benghazi on September 11 is a dramatic example of the potential cost of doing nothing in a moment of crisis. Our GRS team got our gear together and were ready to go within five minutes of receiving the first call for help from the compound. Bob, our chief of base, told us to wait. I'm sure he got that from his superior, our chief of station. I could not say for sure whether that order came from anywhere higher than agency personnel on the ground in Libya. It was frustrating, but it didn't seem crazy at first. The team leader said they needed to come up with a plan, and I hoped he was trying to drum up additional support for us. We had specifically requested air support, a gunship, and an ISR drone, because there were only six of us and we figured we would be outnumbered. We did not know what was being requested, but at first the waiting didn't seem strange, at least for five minutes.

The State Department security people under attack at the consulate were getting frantic on the radio. We knew we were losing the initiative as another ten minutes went by and we got the stand-down order. Another ten minutes elapsed before we finally took matters into our own hands. That delay cost us an additional twenty minutes once we broke orders and took off because we couldn't drive all the way there. We had to get out and fight on foot. It's hard to know what might have happened, but we're very good at what we do and I think if we had been able to get closer to the consulate before the enemy had solidified their position, we might have at least pulled their attention away long enough to let the State Department guys pull their people into a safer position. But it effectively became a forty-five-minute delay between the time of the call and our arrival, and it probably cost Ambassador Stevens and Sean Smith their lives because they died of smoke inhalation. I feel responsible for that. We are military and we are used to doing what our commanders say, but even though we initially thought the wait order was legitimate, we should have bucked it sooner. It is a heavy weight to carry, knowing that following those orders could have cost lives. I carry that burden and know that many veterans struggle with something similar.

Never quitting does not mean refusing to change course if a situation does not feel right or is not going well. Leaders need the confidence and judgment to be able to change direction, even when that means taking a hard right. In Ranger School, if our team is going in the wrong direction and we know it, but the person up front with the compass can't get it done properly, we need to make a change. The decision to do so can't be about that guy's feelings or the original plan. If we let everyone wander in the woods for too long, the leader's inability to navigate is going to affect the operation, as well as everyone else's motivation and attitude. In the best case, guys will get tired and frustrated, and in the worst case, we will compromise the mission. Sometimes pushing forward requires pushing in a different direction.

It might sound counterintuitive, but when I accept that my situation is bad, it helps me stay positive. Pain, discomfort, stress, and pressure are part of life. I try to set my bar to accept and expect that some of the circumstances of my mission might truly suck, and focus my energy on moving through those circumstances as efficiently as possible, if I can't minimize them. I don't waste time feeling sorry for myself. I know that it is more productive to rotate my thinking from "This is so unfair" or "I can't believe this is happening to me" to "This part's done" and "What's next?"

* * *

I found Mountain Phase of Ranger School in Dahlonega, Georgia, to be the most challenging physical environment to work in because we were attacking up a mountainside as opposed to a flat surface or a wooded area. Setting up objective rally points in the woods was also tougher because sometimes we couldn't see a guy two feet away, so it was harder to keep everyone in control and in contact. That was even harder to do at night. On top of that, it was so cold and rainy during my time there that everyone wanted to keep moving to stay warm.

On the third day, we were driven out to the base of Mount Yonah to rappel on a real mountain after practicing our skills at Camp Merrill. After we unloaded, we all got our rucks on, which weighed fifty or sixty pounds, but it didn't feel like much at that point because we had been carrying them so often they had become a part of us. Forced road marches with rucks are hard, and Rangers get strong by doing them regularly. My shoulders, neck, back, and hips were all on fire at first, but my body adjusted. It was getting so cold at Mount Yonah, I actually welcomed my ruck because it trapped some heat on my back.

The RIs stepped off and took off fast, straight up that mountainside, starting a bit of a fuck-fuck game, like that six-mile road march at Cole Range. We walked straight up to the top and a few guys were falling back and falling out, but I thought, "Let's do it, it's on." The walk up the mountain was just the first part of the day. That march wasn't even the point of the day, which would involve rappelling and then training overnight at Mount Yonah. We had brought military tents with us, which was unusual, but it was below freezing. When it was too cold to have guys sleep in their holes, everyone crammed into the tents so close that we called it "nut to butt." There were no sleeping bags; we had just a shell with no insulation and a poncho liner. That was how we slept. The green woolly gloves we wore did not provide a lot of protection against the cold, and my fingers, which I would need to use once we actually started rappelling, felt like sausages. By that time, though, I was getting good at embracing the suck. We got to the top, gave each other high fives, and got started on the training exercise.

* * *

Being confident isn't only about talking myself up or committing to embrace the suck. I know it is important to stay positive for the sake of the people around me. They may need to be motivated or inspired in order to stay on task themselves, or they may simply need to stay calm and under control in order not to become an obstacle that compromises the mission. Staying positive even when I might not feel it is a matter of self-control and confidence.

I remember, our first day back in basic training, our platoon was getting smoked for everything. If someone didn't make his bed the right way, we all did push-ups. If someone screwed up the organization of their drawers, we all did flutter kicks. It was supposed to be like that because they were letting us know that attention to small details matters in the Army. Discipline and obedience matter in the Army, and we were getting the civilian trained out of us from day one. It was stressful because no one was taking us by the hand through any of this, they were just yelling "Get over here!" "Fix it now!" "Get it right!" We had a kid from New York who muttered something about what difference does some of this make, and the drill sergeant called him over:

"You got a problem?" the drill sergeant asked.

"With what?" the kid asked sarcastically.

Their eyes met for a minute, and then the drill sergeant got up from his desk and checked the guy hard. The kid went flying, landed hard, and had a hip pointer for the next two weeks. I don't know if that still happens in basic, but it sure was effective.

A bad attitude is not conducive to team building, and you can bet our group was careful not to display any. That kid learned from his bruised side: he did well and graduated.

WISDOM FROM THE RANGERS
PRINCIPLE EIGHT: CONFIDENCE COMES FROM COMPETENCE

Anticipating a negative event is often worse than actually experiencing it. Your heart starts racing and you let your mind wander, imagining your own version of monsters in the shadows and bumps in the night. You might have a physiological fight-or-flight response. Being able to decode your fear will help you decide on a course of action, and taking action will make you feel better. Sometimes the event itself truly is going to suck, but the quicker you start it, the quicker it's going to be done. The worst thing you can do, in almost every circumstance, is nothing.

Anticipation can be productive if you use it instead of letting it use you. Going through scenarios in your head about what might happen and how you might respond to a given situation can help you prepare and be a good channeling of any adrenaline you might be feeling. Giving in to negative anticipation without strategizing a response is what usually makes people shut down. You have to keep moving and be in the moment. Focus on the task at hand, and get started. That is proactive. That is productive. Then you can start war gaming: What do I have to do? Do we have everything we need to get out of the gate? Do we have all the gear we need? Where are our assets? Are my guys OK? Your questions and concerns will be different and depend on the obstacle you are facing. But start strategizing. Now you're taking action. Now you're being constructive.

In the same way that your confidence can tell you when you need to take the reins and be a leader, it should help you follow when it's appropriate. Being confident means being on top of your game, both tactically and technically, and that means knowing that you don't know everything. When you are secure in your own knowledge, you won't be afraid to ask questions and be willing to learn. Be confident enough to listen to someone who knows more than you, let that person take the initiative when it serves the mission, and be confident enough to share credit when it is due.

Don't panic in a stressful situation. Say you're late on a deadline. Take a deep breath, and start assessing your mission status: "OK, we're behind." Don't look away or engage in wishful thinking or pretend that the situation is not exactly as dire as it is. Start problem solving: "What are we going to do to meet this deadline? What do we need to complete this mission?" That's essentially what was going on in Benghazi, where we were behind the eight ball. Every minute that goes by, you can potentially change your plan. If your plan is good, you don't have to change it, but the point is that you are monitoring conditions and considering your situation. You want to try to stay calm and clear.

Learn how to calm yourself down. I did some aikido martial arts training back in Grand Junction, and in the military we learned lot of combatives to train us for stand-up and ground fighting. Adrenaline can be the chi, the energy you use to fight with, but it needs to go out into your hands and feet so that you can use it to fight. If your mind is spinning out with anxiety or you feel paralyzed by panic, try taking a deep breath, focus, and push that chi energy out to your hands and arms and feet. Think of your adrenaline as a powerful weapon in your arsenal, a kind of super energy. You have to remind yourself that this is normal, that this is how adrenaline works, that you need to get moving, and things will be OK. And they will be.

When you learn how to focus your fear and do it over and over again, you will build competence and your responses will become instinctive. Practice will give you a reflex. Tell yourself that there is no quitting, and you will step out with your best foot forward, with all your assets at their optimum levels. You've been training for this, you know what to do, and you need to get going. If you have ever been an athlete or have committed to getting tough and improving your fitness, you know that the practice of testing yourself in competitive situations when the stakes are lower is constructive. When you give your body a chance to experience the stress and adrenaline you experience in a safe competitive environment, you can remember your responses in other situations and draw upon them.

You might not be confronting physical challenges on the order of RIP or Ranger School, but you will encounter situations that are stressful, that require you to endure, and that require you to make quick or difficult decisions. If you panic, your mind will want to tell you that you can't continue, but you can respond to that thought and redirect it to take action. The most important thing is to keep moving forward. You are less likely to regret an action later than you are to regret not taking action in a moment of crisis.

Once you commit to an action, be confident. This is easier to do if you are properly prepared. If you have been through a similar situation before or, in my case, experienced a particular kind of extreme fatigue, you can be more confident that the decisions you are making are correct for whatever situation you find yourself in. Once you commit to your analysis of what needs to be done and start executing, stay positive.

Your attitude matters. You may not get the kind of feedback on your moods and behavior that the fresh kid from New York got in my unit during basic training, but if you pay attention, you'll notice how people respond to your attitude. When you develop the discipline to stay positive and respectful, even and especially when you are frustrated, you will stay calmer and you will be more likely to keep the people around you working productively toward your common goal as well.

Small things make a big difference in creating a positive, productive atmosphere. Basic manners promote civility. When you say "Yes, sir" or "Yes, ma'am" or call people by their rank, you are showing other people respect, and you will find that it leads to a sense of self-respect. I was raised to be courteous: my family took "please" and "thank you" and "sir" and "ma'am" seriously, so that particular demand of Army life did not seem like a leap for me. But I think it is a leap for some people, and our general sense of civility in social life suffers when we neglect those standards. Basic training also drives home the fact that our physical presence can be a powerful way of communicating a sense of respect. You don't need to stand at attention, but pay attention to how you hold yourself. Your posture matters. When you walk like a professional, with your head up, you are telling people that you feel self-confident, and it helps others have confidence in you. People tend to be more positive and productive when the atmosphere is respectful, and you can have great impact on the atmosphere that surrounds you.

I'm not saying you have to babysit adults, and you don't need to behave like a kindergarten teacher. Sometimes you need to speak loudly or make corrections or recommendations forcefully. In Benghazi, when Boon and I got up onto Building Alpha and the line of sight was not good, we wanted to get to the second building and get the State Department guys off. When we talked about that with each other, we were all loud and it sounded aggressive, but it was cooperative and appropriate for the situation. Being positive doesn't mean you can't ever holler. Just remain calm and respectful, and don't yell for the sake of yelling. And for all my talk of manners, if you want to curse for emphasis, it won't bother me.

When you are in the middle of a crisis, you want your survival skills to kick in. You will feel more confident if you can draw on other ways you have been tested and rely on the knowledge that you are experienced, you have been here before, and you've got this. Are you going to sit in your house and be scared? Are you going to stay stuck in a situation? Commit to taking action. Figure out what makes you feel focused and calm, and practice it. Develop the instincts and judgment you need to counter your fear and make confident decisions. Stay calm and confident as you proceed with your counterattack, not only for yourself but for everyone around you.

Chapter Eleven

RELY ON YOUR BROTHERS

I will never leave a fallen comrade to fall into
the hands of the enemy.
—RANGER CREED

I n a firefight, I have to trust my brothers with my life, and they trust theirs to me. Circumstances don't matter; there are no excuses. I still like being around other veterans because I know that no matter what our service experience was, we've all been willing to make the ultimate sacrifice. I think a lot of people like me miss the camaraderie that develops between soldiers and find comfort being around people who have been through that experience. We all learn how to be part of a team and to depend on each other in training, and many of us become privileged to see that brotherhood is a powerful force under fire. When I say brotherhood, by the way, that includes women who serve. Brotherhood has nothing to do with gender in my mind.

When things started going wrong on September 11 in Benghazi, our Annex security team banded together. Dave

"Boon" Benton, Mark "Oz" Geist, John "Tig" Tiegen, Jack Silva, Tyrone "Rone" Woods, and I were all former special operators or Marines and experienced security contractors, but we had not been together as a team for all that long before September 11. Boon and I were good friends, as were Jack and Rone, and Tig and Boon had worked together before, but we were assigned to Benghazi individually.

Some of the work we have to do overseas has to be clandestine, which means we do not have the same kinds of resources or support that a conventional military mission would have. It is just the team on the ground and our survival depends on being able to work as a unit. The members of our group in Benghazi developed respect and trust for one another during the day-to-day operations and would often hang out together during downtime or after hours, playing video games, talking, and sharing meals. It was so comfortable that Boon, Rone, and I extended our time in Benghazi to help with the ambassador's visit, even though we were all scheduled to return home in early September. It's great when I can develop friendships with people on a team, but when it happens I recognize it as a bonus. I was experienced enough to appreciate it in Benghazi.

Working as a group can be hard, and I have been in situations where a GRS team or a military unit does not have the same natural, cohesive feeling that we developed in Benghazi. That's to be expected. Even among people who have shared interests, goals, or training experiences, our individual motivations and personalities may be very different. Sometimes I have encountered members of a group that don't have the skills or attitude I thought we needed. And sometimes there are people who just plain bug me. In my line of work, I might not even be able to get away from guys who are driving me crazy at the end of the day because we have to sleep in the same room or tent. But when a team functions properly, everyone has a part to play. In the same way that I need to have a clear sense of myself, I need to have a clear sense of the people in my unit and how to help us all work effectively together.

PUT THE MISSION FIRST

My earliest experiences of being on a team were probably on the football field or playing organized sports. As any team athlete knows, not everyone can be a superstar, and team success depends on the ability to coordinate everyone's strengths and cover one another's weaknesses during a game. Playing sports was also probably my first opportunity to see how people can put aside their differences in service to a larger mission, such as winning a game or a season. By the time I started playing football at Dixie State Junior College in St. George, Utah, I had many years of practice learning how to be a good team player. But Dixie was interesting. Dixie's football team was very good, and many of the players hoped to move on to Division 1 schools. The team I played on turned out to be a mix of rival gang members from different locations and sects as well as redneck boys who had grown up on local farms. We had guys from the West Coast Bloods from Los Angeles playing with Donna Street Crips from Las Vegas and Tongan Crips from Inglewood, California and Salt Lake City, Utah. There were big kids from Hawaii and a huge bear of a guy from Alaska. Everyone was out of his neighborhood, thrown together in the locker room, and everyone wanted to win.

I was new and I was small relative to a lot of the other guys. Also, even though I am half Mexican, I am also half Basque, and when you look at me, I look Anglo. So there I was, the newbie playing wide receiver, going against tough guys that could be going to D1 schools. During my second practice, I came across the middle of the field, and one guy, a Donna Street Crip from north Las Vegas, closed in on me and knocked me hard on my ass. I popped back up, pissed as hell, and ran back to the huddle. The quarterback looked at me and asked if I was OK. I met his eyes.

"Just throw me the fucking ball again."

He nodded. "All right, all right, dude."

After that I was fine. No questions. No one messed with me, and I found that the players did not mess with one another. The guys on that team were all close, even though our backgrounds were pretty different. And I just loved it. I thrived on the competition and enjoyed working with good players. I actually got a scholarship the next year based on my football performance, made honorable mention all-American, all-conference, and all-region, and, I'm not going to lie, I started to get a little full of myself. But my teammates kept me, and one another, in check, and I saw how a sense of mission can bring people together. I remember one of my teammates saying about another, "You know, if Chuckie walked down the block in my neighborhood at home, he'd be dead. But here, I play with him." There was no animosity between them, on the field or off; he was just acknowledging a reality. The shared goal of being a winning football team was a starting point.

In the military, the stakes are higher, and the need to trust and rely on the team rises to another level. In high school and college, I was not living with my teammates 24/7. In the Army, I was rarely alone. I had very little privacy, and everyone was being tested in front of one another, and sometimes I failed in front of my brothers. We were all failing, separately and together, and it didn't matter whether a particular failure belonged to one of us in particular, because we would all be punished for it. We were all getting the civilian trained out of us, we were all being yelled at, we were all getting smoked doing push-ups and flutter kicks. The methods and discipline might seem harsh, but they were meant to make us strong. The shared punishments also helped us bond as a unit and helped us start to learn brotherhood.

TELL THE TRUTH

During basic training at Fort Benning, learning drill and ceremony was one of the first ways we started learning teamwork. We were learning military bearing and standard commands, such as right face and left face, and how to move in an orderly, uniform manner. This is routine stuff, and it seems as though it should be easy. But all forty members of the unit need to be uniform and the commands and movements are precise. We would come to dread drill and ceremony because there would always be one or two guys screwing up a movement and the drill sergeants would use it as a place to set examples. We would be out on the hot asphalt in full uniform, doing flutter kicks and mountain climbers until the drill sergeants got tired of watching us. It doesn't sound like such a big deal, but having to work out in full uniform when it is hot and humid as hell while someone yells "Unfuck yourselves!" or "Fix your shit right now!" creates a complicated dynamic.

First, it brings everyone who is suffering together in shared misery. Second, it creates an incentive for guys to help one another. If anyone messes up, everyone shares the pain. So we began to come together to help the less coordinated among us. Now, that help was not always delivered in the most diplomatic, sensitive way; "Get your shit together" might have been one of the nicer things someone might hear. Guys were cursing. People got mad at each other, but it didn't turn into bullying, or at least it didn't when I was there. It took a while to get it right, but eventually we began working as a unit. And we cheered each other on when we finally moved successfully in tandem, because the drill sergeants did not.

The drill sergeants or RIP cadre would not correct one another in front of us, but we could see them working as a team, too, protecting one another and helping one another to perform at their best. Sometimes the drill sergeants would bang on our Kevlar helmets with a little paddle and scream, "Get your shit right!" or "Get your fucking shit squared away!" It wasn't like a beating, more of a smack on the head with something resembling a Ping-Pong paddle. I remember once watching a very frustrated drill sergeant seem like he was about to lose his cool and another instructor meeting his eyes and motioning for him to take a break. He did. There were no words needed. Leaders need to walk away sometimes, too, and they are also brothers and members of a team that look out for one another.

COVER ONE ANOTHER

Teammates need to cover one another which means we need to understand one another's strengths and weaknesses. If there is a weakness in the system or the team that everyone can anticipate, we can be prepared to jump in for one another.

Road marches, which require both individual endurance and group coordination, are a key part of basic training, the RIP, the 75th Ranger Regiment, and Ranger School. We need to stay about five meters apart when we are moving, in case bullets start flying out in the field, but we also need to maintain pace and formation. The requirement is that our unit march in uniform, but we can't be too close together. When one guy starts to slow down or fall out, eighty guys are affected, especially toward the end of the line. When that starts happening, the guys at the end have to run to keep up and close the gap. If someone can't keep up, we call him a blue falcon. That's a polite way of saying that he is fucking his buddy.

Sometimes in basic, we might be able to carry someone's ruck and literally lighten his load for a while, or I might be able to hold an arm out behind the ruck of the guy in front of me and physically steady or push someone forward who was slowing down. A guy could get away with that kind of support once in a while in basic. But in RIP, the marches were graded events and everyone had to be able to keep up and carry their own fifty-to-sixty-pound rucksack for the full three hours. In that case, all we could do was motivate one another verbally. It was great to see guys pushing one another. Some guys might say, "You got this" to a buddy who was faltering. I was usually more like a caveman: "Motherfucker, you better get your ass in gear. You are screwing everyone up in the back." Even if it might have sounded like we were yelling at one another, we were all working together. If someone can't do it, he can't do it; let him drop out. But sometimes people have the potential and they just need a little motivation. By the later phases of training, the physically weaker guys had pretty much gone, so most people dropping at that stage either really didn't want to be there or hadn't found their mental toughness.

GET TO KNOW ONE ANOTHER

Be realistic. No one likes everyone all the time. It's OK. We don't have to like everybody; we just have to get along. As long as someone is not a weak link, even if our differences are substantial, we must find ways of working together. Mark "Oz" Geist and I are extremely different in our temperaments and our interests. But he is good at what he does, he always planned his ops well, and I respected him as a capable colleague. I was glad to be on a team with him on September 11, and I credit him, along with the other guys who fought alongside me, for my survival. I do not spend my energy trying to make everyone my best friend. It's important to be myself and let other people be themselves.

There is a lot on the line in my job, and having a sense of humor helps me deal with the pressure. People take themselves too damn seriously most of the time, and I just can't go along with it. Or maybe I'm just juvenile. But it's who I am. I was standing up on the rooftop early in the morning of September 12 in Benghazi when Bub, the two Delta Force operators, and our other GRS Team from Tripoli got in, and I said, " Hey, guys, welcome, it's a hell of a party we're having here today, love to see you, glad you're here." They all thought it was funny that I greeted them like they were arriving at a cool social event, and some of them laughed. One of the guys was shaking his head and said, "Same old Tanto."

I am good at my job, but I am not the most professional or politically correct guy. I like to laugh. It makes me feel good to lighten the moment. When I was on the roof in Benghazi and they asked me if I needed anything and I asked for a stripper, that was just me. It made people laugh. If I can keep things as light as they can be, maybe people won't go into the black. I laugh so I don't lose my mind.

Sometimes I would be walking by a security camera on our base and I might break into a crazy dance for a few seconds and then just stop and keep walking as if nothing had happened, just to mess with the static security guys who were monitoring the cameras. Or I might gaslight a buddy, moving something minor from one part of his locker to another, back and forth. If someone left a piece of gear unattended, I might freeze it in a jug of water. Sometimes there's a little something in it for me. It probably won't surprise you to know that a lot of GRS guys like to play video games during their downtime. In Benghazi, we played a lot of Call of Duty on Xbox during our off-hours; we used to call it "tactical training." During a different posting, the team I was with loved to play Halo. Now, I'm bad at Halo and I hated that they monopolized the TV with it, so one day I took the disk and hid it. Halo was so popular with the regular Army guys that it was always sold out at the PX and you couldn't easily round up another copy. The guys were in fits. I let that go on for a good thirty days and enjoyed every minute of it.

* * *

I am not above playing practical jokes on outsiders, either. My friend and fellow Ranger from the 75th Regiment Alex Saenz and I were in Afghanistan together, and sometimes we had to take people to the airport. It was a dangerous area, so we couldn't just put people on some shuttle bus. It was an important security precaution, but on some level it felt silly: two highly trained combat professionals driving a van, taking people to the airport. So Alex and I would have a little fun. We'd pick people up and whisper loudly to each other in front of them, like "Do you know what this weapon is? I don't think I've ever seen one of these before."

"I don't know, man, I think it's like an M6 or something?"

"Hey, do you know how to use this radio?"

We would drive, and we would goof and enjoy watching the people in the backseat stiffen up for a minute. But when it was time to get busy, we were serious. People knew they could count on us, and they let us have our fun.

Yes, I can take a joke, too. Alex and I used to play practical jokes on each other all the time. I remember one where I came back from an outer base and he said that our static security guys were short and asked if I would help them out by volunteering to take the 1:00 a.m. shift for manning a guard post. Of course I said sure. So I got out there at one in the morning and was sitting with a local who couldn't speak English, but that was not unusual, so I just took my post and hung out. After more than an hour, one of the guys on the team called me on the radio to ask where I was. I told him I was taking a shift at the guard tower, and he started laughing. He said, "I can't let this go on. You know this is a joke, right?" Alex got me. I was out there until two in the morning pulling guard when I didn't have to be! I was laughing and pissed and already thinking about how I was going to get his ass back. I found a ham sandwich and an open tin of anchovies and shoved them way down in his M4 pouches and his MET pouch between his medical supplies so he would have to dig deep to find it. He didn't find it until it really started stinking about a month later. He thought it was hilarious, although he did give me a judo kick the day after he found it and nearly broke my damn shin.

As good as Alex was at giving me a hard time, he also always had my back. We were together at Ranger Battalion during my first rotation there, so when I went back into the Army and had to go through training again, Alex was there as a private. When the other newbies were leaning on me and wearing me out, he looked out for me. One night he pinned a note on my bunk while I was sleeping. It read, "All you motherfuckers leave Kris alone, he's tired."

When we were at basic together, Alex just got punished in the beginning because he was not physically strong. He was a big kid, but he had to make himself tough through hard work and drive. He did it, and he became a better Ranger than me. He made E6P, staff sergeant promotable, in Ranger Battalion before becoming a contractor. We haven't been through any firefights together, but we've been on ops together in Afghanistan and I always felt we could take on the world together and win. He is the hardest worker you will ever meet, a tough guy who continued to deploy while fighting leukemia.

BE DEPENDABLE

Other guys tend to expect positivity from me and count on me to keep things light. I'm generally happy to oblige. But I have my down moments, and I've been lucky to be able to turn to Matt Selcke at those times. Matt and I played football together at Grand Junction High School and Mesa State University, and we enlisted at the same time. I was lucky to go through basic training with him and know that there was someone I could trust from the get-go. Matt has had my back any time I've needed him and has been a relentlessly positive and reassuring presence in my life. Which is not the same as saying he's a saint. In fact, he can be superstealthy and is the type of guy who would risk getting in trouble for smuggling candy into the barracks. A few months into basic, we came in from a long ruck march and I was worn all the way out. As I was falling asleep, I felt a pat on my head and smelled something sweet. I opened my mouth to say "What the—" and Matt shoved a bunch of Skittles into my mouth. He had smuggled those Skittles in from the PX, and it was a violation to have any personal food like that in the bay. He was already walking smoothly away by the time I opened my eyes.

Matt is the person I called when I was feeling so hopeless about my marriage and my life in Colorado. He showed up. It was a good feeling to know that I had someone in my life I could count on like that, and I try to make sure that others can count on me when they need to.

KEEP MOVING, KEEP TALKING, TRY TO STAY POSITIVE

Did we have a perfect plan in Benghazi? No. Did we even have a plan? Not really. But we communicated with one another. We trusted one another. We needed to get out of the gate, assess what was going on, and adjust on the fly using our experience and our instincts. That's what I believe our CIA people did not get. Lives were on the line: we could question and doubt, but we could not freeze. We had to make the best decisions we could, fill and flow, adjust on the fly, and keep moving and talking.

The final phase of Ranger School takes place at Camp Rudder in Elgin, Florida, and is called Swamp Phase or Florida Phase. During Ranger School, the whole squad rates each other during each phase, on a scale of 1 to 8. I did not see my peer scores until the whole thing was over but would come to find out that I earned ninety-something percent in Benning Phase, eighty-something percent in Mountain Phase, and seventy-something percent in Florida Phase. I think that is a fair reflection of my mood and attitude as the training went on. As I got hungrier and more tired, I became crankier and less likely to lend a hand to my brothers. By Florida Phase, I was pushing the limits of my endurance.

I did Florida Phase during the winter and it was cold and miserable. Some big storms came through during our training, but we did not deviate from our mission. One night we were told to dig our holes—our fighting positions—as deep as possible at about 10:00 p.m. and settle in. I looked around at about one in the morning as a mean wind whipped above me and watched the sky flash with lightening. I couldn't see the RIs, which was not unusual because they are trying to grade you surreptitiously, but something felt eerie. When they came back to raise us at 6:00 a.m., I knew something was off. We had gotten almost five hours of sleep, which was the longest we had slept in weeks. Sure enough, two small tornados had touched down that night. But we pressed on. Everyone was trying to work together to get things done properly, but everyone was exhausted, we all stank, and guys were complaining more.

I was a weapons squad leader on one of the ops where we assaulted a makeshift village, and it went well. I briefed part of the op order and understood that at that point we were learning how to delegate responsibilities. Everyone was hurting, and guys were tense about getting their "go"s. One last op had two guys from an Operational Detachment Alpha (ODA) team who needed their primary "go"s. I had my "go"s, but the RIs made the tactically stronger guys who had already passed take on leadership positions to assist with assaulting the airfield on the op.

We did a lot of direct action training missions in Florida, and a plan would never work out the way we wanted it to go. But we had to keep moving forward, and we were getting better at working as a team, even if we were complaining. Everyone's skills were improving, so a mission could still be successful and accomplished even when it did not go according to plan. Nothing was ever carried out with one hundred percent efficiency, yet, as we moved through the woods, I could feel the change. Certain things felt easy. I almost didn't need my compass, because I could terrain associate now and walk and feel oriented by the hills and ravines around me. But we were still learning. I got too aggressive with the assault and pushed my squad out too far ahead of the squad we were supposed to be supporting.

We kept pushing forward, and we radioed the other guys and kind of reversed position. I immediately regrouped and asked them to cover us instead, so we communicated and still carried out the attack.

Our last march in Florida was twelve or thirteen miles. I grabbed the machine gun first and put a sleeping bag on the back of my rucksack. The sleeping bag was annoying because the squad always had to carry one around in case someone got hypothermia, but no one ever used it. I didn't take the time to pack it properly, I just bungeed it in a ball to the top of my ruck. I looked like a hunchback. The machine gun could not get seated right because of the mess on my backpack. It hurt as soon as I started moving. My shoulders were dying. I was worn out, and at about mile six, I started to fall back. I was trying to step it up, but my legs just did not want to go. I kept focusing on the pain in my shoulders, which was radiating down into my lower back. My mind was starting to quit. I was fighting it, telling myself "You've come this far, don't you dare quit," but my shoulders were screaming. I stepped out to try to adjust the backpack, and of course the RIs gave me a hard time: "Step back up! If you step out, you're done!" I thought, "Shit, I am almost done. I've got about six miles left in this march and then I'm done with this whole damn thing, but I'm not going to be able to make it." At that moment, one of the IOBC guys I had been helping along the way approached me and said, "Paronto, give me the machine gun."

"Are you kidding me?" I was incredulous, embarrassed, and relieved. He was not one of the stronger guys. He smiled.

"You've been helping me this whole way." He nodded. He was right and way more gracious than I had been toward the end when I was giving him a hand.

I handed it over, and he gave me his M4. Just that little bit of pressure off my shoulder changed my mental state, and I was able to step it out. I stayed behind him and was prepared to help push him along, but he never faltered.

At about a half mile from the end of the march, I could have sworn I saw a shooting star sail across the sky above the road. I was so discombobulated, I wasn't sure if it was real. Some guys said they saw it, others didn't, and many were too exhausted to speak. Finally we got in. We were done.

We turned in our weapons and were given a hot dog party. I remember I ate three hot dogs and three full-sized Snickers bars and drank three Pepsis. We were eating these outside in the cold and my hands were shaking, but it tasted like the best meal I had ever eaten. We were let in to get cleaned up. I took my first shower after ten days in the field, and it felt like a hot power wash.

That night, they told us to wait for our roster number to be called to find out if we had passed Ranger School or not. It was the whole company, so that was a long night. We had all been sleeping in freezing foxholes for ten days, but everyone stayed awake. Everyone was too anxious waiting for their own numbers to be called. They called my number at 2:00 or 3:00 a.m., and I went in and sat down with two RIs. One looked at me and just said, "Welcome to the brotherhood. You're a Ranger."

"I passed?" That's what I said. I knew I had earned my "go"s, and I had felt fairly confident about passing, but I was still overwhelmed. The memories of everything I had gone through in order to get to that moment flashed across my mind as if I was looking at them through one of those old Viewmasters at light speed. This had been my mission for so long, and I was overcome at having finally completed it. Even today, I can get choked up thinking about it. The RIs reviewed my scores and reminded me that not everyone was going to make it, so I should keep my emotions in check when I went back outside. I remember thinking it was cool that even in that moment of great personal triumph, I was being reminded to think of my brothers.

WISDOM FROM THE RANGERS
PRINCIPLE NINE: TRUST YOUR BROTHERS

There is a limit to everyone's patience, but it is easier to let your teammates be themselves when you know you can count on them. I think that's part of why I get away with some of my nonsense, because the people I work with know I can pivot and get deadly serious when they need me to be. You need to find the people in your life whom you can count on and be a person they can trust. When you say you're going to do something, do it. The last things you are going to have in this world are your balls and your word, that's it. If you don't have those, you've got nothing.

Accept your brothers for who they are, but be honest with one another. In the military, feedback is very direct. When I was doing a crappy job, the leadership let me know, and they didn't put a premium on protecting my feelings. That is not a bad thing, and it made me mentally tough. When someone gives you negative feedback, your feelings might be a little hurt and you might feel bad, but you also learn that you are still here. You survive it. And you can get and give positive feedback, too. You can pat a guy on the back and say "You're doing fine" just as easily as "Get your shit together." As guys start to become more of a team, they support one another. If a guy made a mistake in Ranger School, people might say to him on the side, "You got this." When I have been a leader, I've tried to make it a point to say "Keep it up" or "Keep improving" when it made sense.

It isn't always appropriate to be as harsh and direct in the civilian world as one would be in the military, but the idea of receiving feedback and discipline in the moment and not during an evaluation two months later, has wide application. You learn to identify errors and correct practices immediately. You also learn how to handle criticism directly and gracefully, even if it is delivered without sensitivity. You will develop trust with your brothers when you are honest with one another. And when you get a compliment from a guy who you know will tell you a harsh truth, it will mean something.

Sometimes it's hard to be straight if someone is messing up, especially when that person is struggling or if you know the truth is going to hurt his or her feelings. But you're usually not doing each other any favors by staying silent. Being straight with your teammates and the other people in your life will make you all stronger.

———————————————————

Chapter Twelve

HAVE FAITH

I . . . will fight with all my might.
—RANGER CREED

Greater love hath no man than this, that he
lay down his life for his friends.
—JOHN 15:13

I am a Christian. I am a sinner, like everyone else. As you have read in these pages, I am deeply fallible. But I have faith that God takes care of me and forgives me when I ask for forgiveness. I accept that whatever is going on in my life, whether it is good, bad, violent, or beautiful, is where God wants me to be. There is a prayer I always remember, from a wartime Bible that was given to me by a Ranger buddy back in 2003. It's called Prayer Before Battle, and it ends, "If I die on this battlefield today, may I die at peace with You." I remember being ticked off the first time I read it, thinking "God, why are you telling me this? I don't want to die in battle." But I talked about it with my pastor and he said, "Kris, that's not what this means. Think about it. God has you in a situation. Accept it. Accept where you're at and do the best you can. That is what God wants you to do."

I believe that I am a warrior for the United States. I believe that Rangers are warriors for one another and our nation, and also warriors for God. Some terrorists say they are warriors for God. But I don't blow myself up and kill little girls and women indiscriminately. I've never shot at anybody who hasn't been shooting at me, and there have been times when I held off shooting because the enemy was taking cover in houses or locations we knew had children in them. So you tell me who are God's warriors.

* * *

The CIA changed many of its security procedures overseas after a suicide attack in 2009 in Khost, Afghanistan, that killed ten people and injured six others who were working for and with the CIA at Camp Chapman. An al-Qaeda operative who had been in talks to allegedly provide intelligence to the agency detonated a bomb sewn into his clothing after being allowed to enter the base before being searched. I was working in Kandahar the following year, and we were prescreening visitors to our facility in a special outbuilding. If anyone was going to get blown up, it would be us, the GRS Team. One morning we were asked to search a Taliban member who was being cultivated to work with the agency. It was his initial meeting on-site as a potential source. He was nervous, had never been searched before, and was not being cooperative when we asked him to raise his arms and empty his pockets. Our interpreter was trying to explain the purpose of the standard search, but the guy was resistant. My partner was getting agitated and told the interpreter to tell him to turn his pockets inside out and get his arms up in the air or this was not happening, which only seemed to distress the guy.

After much back-and-forth, the interpreter explained that the guy did not want us to touch the small Koran that he kept in his pants. I pulled out my pocket-sized New Testament, laid it on the table, and invited him to pick it up. I asked the interpreter to tell him what it was and to tell him, "We are the same. We believe in the same God." He looked back and forth between the Bible and me. He looked stunned. He picked up my Bible and turned the pages slowly. I'm sure he could not read English, but he could see where I had marked the well-worn pages, and he seemed to be considering something. I asked the interpreter to tell him, "There is no disrespect here. Would you trust me to come into your house like this?" He understood. And he lifted his arms and let me pat him down. I asked him, through the interpreter, to pick up his Koran and turn the pages so that we could look through it together. I don't know anything else about how that member of the Taliban understands the obligations of his religious beliefs or his life's path, but the evidence of my own faith enabled him to cooperate with me.

* * *

Faith helps me to be fearless. It is so much easier to let go of fear or anger and embrace adversity when I accept that my path is the one I am supposed to be on. Acceptance is not an excuse to quit. Acceptance means that I know there is not only an obstacle before me but also a purpose. When the battle in Benghazi started on September 11, I was ready to accept it. I had been deploying for more than ten years at that point. I saw the firefight going, and I ran toward it because I accepted the fact that God had placed me on that battlefield at that moment.

Between firefights in Benghazi, at around one in the morning, Boon and I were sitting in our fighting position up on the roof of Building B. We knew how outnumbered we were, and I was still war gaming in my mind and thinking about the enemy coming back at us with heavier weapons. I spoke my mind. "If they come back at us with anything bigger than RPGs or AKs, or they come with a technical mounted, bro, we're not going to be able to fight that off. We don't have the weaponry for that."

"Yeah, I know," Boon agreed.

"If they do, me and you, we're going to have to get down off this building and start getting out of this compound. We're going to have to move toward them. And we're going to have to attack them direct."

"Yup," Boon said, nodding. "I know."

I was telling him that if we had to get off that roof together, we were not coming back. We knew that. I was telling him that we might die together that night, and he just said, "Yup." He smiled at me. Boon and I had been together a long time, in Iraq, Afghanistan, and Libya. Neither of us had to say, "I'll give my life for you, brother." I think we both knew that we had each other's back. And he knew me well enough to know that I believed that as long as we were doing the right thing, God would take care of us.

My faith that God protects us, as long as we're trying to help and willing to sacrifice ourselves, doesn't mean I believe He is going to keep me alive. It means I believe He has us all on our own paths for a purpose and that I will accept mine. No one wants to die, but my life is not any more important than Boon's or that of any other soldier, Marine, airman, or seaman who might be standing next to me. Being willing to sacrifice for God, country, and family is part of my training and my faith.

I felt that confidence and strength throughout the night in Benghazi. When we got hit hard at the compound during the second attack, Boon and I were initially taking cover by one of the State Department vehicles near the front lawn. I knew I could get a better angle from the other side of the driveway but that it would require stepping right out into the firing line. The State guys were ready to get out of there, too; they needed me to peel off their car in order to move. We could hear the *snapsnap* of the gunfire past our ears like someone cracking a whip. It's hard to describe that sound and the feel of the high-velocity rounds cutting through the air. We were returning fire, but I had to move across the road without cover in order to get offensive; there was no other way to do it. I stepped out and started moving, taking a knee right out in the open. It's hard to explain, but as I was shooting, I felt protected. I knew God had me. I felt a physical sense of protection, like a warm golden blanket, wrapped around me like a cocoon. I could feel that God was with me. I don't normally feel like God has his hand right on top of me, but I did while I was shooting at that moment. I fought as hard as I could, trying to take out anything that looked like it was coming through the back gate.

As I was shooting, I was running out of ammunition and having a hard time getting my extra magazine out of my shorts pockets. I saw an AK-47 barrel come into my peripheral vision, no more than ten feet away. It was firing so close to my head that it blew my eardrum out, and that hurt really bad. I looked right quick, and there was a short, middle-aged Libyan guy who looked like he'd just gotten off work, in a button-down shirt and nice slacks. He took a knee next to me, picked up his AK-47, and nodded and smiled at me as he continued shooting toward the back gate. "Where did this guy come from?" I wondered, grateful and amused, "God just put a Libyan angel right next to me." It was amazing. Then Boon came screaming around the corner and took a knee on my other side. He knew I needed help. Someone else might see it differently, but I felt as though God was looking out for us and maybe he had a sense of humor about it.

GRATITUDE

One way we can strengthen a sense of faith in our lives is by cultivating a sense of gratitude. I can be on a battlefield and think "This is awful" or I can think "Yes, I get to be on this

Earth. I get to be here, right now. I get to be of service, in a situation most people might only see in the movies." When I make that shift, my world opens up, and it doesn't have to happen in a crisis situation.

The ruck marches in basic and in Ranger training were not dire, but they were always painful. Sometimes we had to get ready to go at about 4:30 on those mornings, because the march takes the place of PT but lasts longer, so we had to start earlier. When we set out, everyone was already tired and we all knew we had a full day of training afterward. We'd have our BDU uniforms and our fifty-pound rucksacks, and sometimes we had to wear our awkward, heavy Kevlar helmets. We would take off like that and start walking at a fifteen-minute-mile pace. I remember heading out on one march where we were going off post to what's called Fryar Field Drop Zone. I was working hard to walk fast, but I was also looking around. It is beautiful to look up at the stars in the Fort Benning sky at that hour of the morning. It's called early-morning nautical twilight, and it's awesome. We were a little sore from the week's training, but I remember noticing that my feet had toughened up a bit and appreciating that my boots were broken in. I wasn't consciously trying to feel grateful on that march, but by paying close attention to each moment and noticing those small good things—the stars, the sky, my boots, and my relative comfort—was a way of counting my blessings.

Blessings do not have to be dramatic. One of the side benefits of being tested and going through hard times is the ability to recognize relative comfort when it's over. When I was an untabbed Ranger, if I wasn't doing an op, I was getting messed with. It wasn't personal; that was just how it was for all untabbed Rangers. I might be walking along minding my own business and a tabbed guy could call, from hundreds of yards away, "Hey, Ranger Paronto, get over here." I'd have to come hustling. "Why are you over here? I didn't call you! What are you doing over here?" was the inevitable answer when I reported. Another favorite game of the Ranger Cadre at Cole Range involved some trees at the end of a large open area the size of a football field. They would tell us to go run and get them a branch; we would run and bring one, they would find something wrong with it and then they'd send us back and forth over 100 meters for a different branch until they thought of something else fun.

There was no place to hide from any of that. In fact, if someone was found hiding or really screwed up, or showed any kind of smart attitude at all, he might have to hang from a pull-up bar until his hands started to rip up and bleed. The tabbed Rangers made it suck, and we had to embrace the misery or quit. I had to tell myself that if I couldn't handle it, I would fail out in the field. It did reset my bar for appreciating positives afterward. When I get frustrated today, Ranger training has given me a whole arsenal of memories that I can call upon to put things into perspective: At least I'm not sweating or starving. At least no one is messing with me, making me run 100 meters back and forth to grab a branch just for the fun of it. At least I'm not getting blown up by 81 mm mortars. Things could be worse.

LOOK UP AND OUT

Many people can find a sense of strength and connection to something larger than themselves when they are outdoors in nature. I was a winter Ranger when I went to Ranger School, training in the woods of the Tennessee Valley Divide during Mountain Phase. It was below freezing at night, and I can remember the feeling of the cracked skin on my hands rubbing against the wool gloves we wore, which didn't do much to keep us warm. We had to climb, gripping the cold rocks of Mount Yonah with our cut-up hands, and then rappel back down the mountain on sling ropes that we had to create with D-rings and tie off ourselves. My body would shake trying to warm itself, and the ends of my frozen fingers were splitting around each cuticle. The tips of my fingers still hurt when it is very cold today. My body would shake, trying to warm itself. On one trip up, my fingers were so clumsy and numb that I snapped them in the D-ring I was using to create my seat. It hurt like hell, and I stood there and flashed on the thought that I wasn't even through the halfway point of Ranger School. But there was beauty even in that miserable moment. I was waiting on the guy in front of me to go down, and I just stood there looking out at the clear blue stillness of the sky and had a moment of appreciation for God's work. I allowed myself a moment of wonder and awe, and it gave me strength.

FAITH CLARIFIES YOUR VALUES

"Greater love hath no man than this, that he lay down his life for his friends" (John 15:13) is one of my favorite passages from the Bible. That is the law that all veterans live by, overseas and in combat. That is the law our team lived by on September 11 in Benghazi. That is the law we always live by, but that night it became visible for the whole world to see.

Every member of our team was trained to respect our commanders and follow orders. When our leaders told us to stand down, we waited. We waited, geared up and ready to go, and listened to the sounds of a firefight in the distance. We listened to Alec Henderson on the radio, asking, "GRS, where are you? GRS, where are you at? GRS, we need you. GRS, we're taking heavy fire. GRS, you swore you'd get here." I could feel that my frustration was shared by our whole team, and I could feel an energy changing, almost charging the air around us. We knew we needed to take over. When you are clear about your own values, you know when it is time to stop listening to man's law and start listening to God's law. My other teammates might have come at the decision to buck orders differently, but that is how I made my judgment. Leaders take the hard right instead of the easy wrong. Having faith helped me know what was right and gave me the strength to take that action.

GOD CAN SET YOU ON A NEW PATH

When I came back to the United States after Benghazi and saw the story of September 11 being misconstrued, lied about, and covered up, I became so angry. My frustration grew as our experience became politicized, and I started to think that I hated my country. Some people were surprised when I signed up to go back and do GRS work in Yemen after having survived the attack on Benghazi. But I wanted to be with other contractors, guys I knew I could trust. And I was keeping in contact with my brothers from Benghazi, who were all struggling with the same feelings of demoralization. It was cathartic to set the record straight by working with Mitchell Zuckoff to write our book, *13 Hours*, but when I started to do media appearances to support the book, I began to hate my life even more. My training had prepared me to be a Ranger, not a public figure. I felt like I was saying "Hey, look at me, look at us, look at what we did." I felt deeply uncomfortable. The book reignited the partisan attention and agenda shifting around the Benghazi attack that had disturbed me in the first place.

We were at a book signing at a Barnes & Noble in Dallas, Texas, one night that got a particularly large turnout. I should have been grateful for the crowd, but I was exhausted and low. I always try to stay and sign every book and talk with anyone who wants to connect with me, and by the time I walked out of that event I was miserable and wondering if it was all pointless. I felt like giving up. But God did not lose faith in me. He brought me an older lady, who approached me at the airport.

"Are you Tanto?"

"Yes, what do you want?" was what came out of my mouth. I immediately envisioned my dad's belt coming across my backside while he told my conscience, "Boy, you'd better respect a woman!" I turned, looked her in the eye, and adjusted my tone.

"I'm sorry," I said. "Yes, ma'am, I'm Tanto."

"You were in Benghazi"

"Yes, ma'am."

"I believe you." She looked me in eye and nodded. "Keep telling your story."

I don't know that woman's name, and I've never seen her again. She has no idea what she did for me by telling me "I believe in you" at that particular moment, when I needed to hear it so badly. I believe that God was telling me that one battle was finished and I was being set on a new path to fight a different battle. Roger that. I accept that. I miss being overseas. I miss the guys I trained and worked with. But I know that this is where I need to be right now.

ACCEPTANCE

By the last night of our field training exercises (FTX) in basic training, I was exhausted. After spending a sleepless week out on a big range in Fort Benning, my platoon had successfully executed the exercises, and I knew I would pass the FTX and graduate from basic. There was a light at the end of the tunnel and I did feel tougher, as if I was becoming a real soldier. But I had blown the Officer Candidate Test and was in pieces about the state of my marriage. All I wanted to do was talk to my wife in person. I wasn't sure what I was going to do after basic, and I was beat tired. It had been a clear day, but, as night fell, the sky became dark and still and a sudden storm rolled in. We had no tents or sleeping bags, we had just been lying on the ground with poncho liners at night. As the rain poured down, guys were moving to take what cover they could, but I remember that I didn't want to move. The rain was coming down in sheets, but I just stayed in the field and let it drench me. I felt a deep sense of calm, not exactly happy or sad but still and peaceful. It felt like a moment of radical acceptance: This is my life. I love it and I hate it, but this is my life. Bring it on.

WISDOM FROM THE RANGERS
PRINCIPLE TEN: GOD WILL NEVER QUIT ON YOU

Every one of us needs faith. When you are confronting adversity or trying to make changes in your life, it will help to have a belief in something or someone greater than yourself. Faith can be a powerful source of strength, inspiration, and comfort, and it can help guide you to develop clarity about your life's purpose and your own values. Faith is not the same as hope. Hope and optimism are important, but faith is a kind of trust that will be the core of your persistence. Faith is a belief, a metaphysical energy that will give you strength and free you to take action. When you start to problem solve and take action, your path can continue to unfold.

Try to take time to reflect on and be grateful for your blessings. I promise you that you have them, no matter how dire your situation is or how low you might be feeling. Most of us have a remarkable ability to take things for granted. It's like how you probably never think about your ankles, but then if you twist one hard, you can't think of anything else every time you take a step. There are probably a few conditions you enjoy that you are taking for granted. Take a minute to appreciate them. There's a good chance you can feel part of something larger, however you choose to understand it, when you give yourself a moment to be still in the natural world. That might help put your troubles into perspective and help you hang on. You might be miserable, but you're not going to quit.

Having faith can also help you find purpose when you are in pain. Painful feelings can be a message that something is not working in your life and you need to make a change in the same way that physical pain can alert you that something might be wrong with your body. I did not want to accept the pain of my marriage ending. I paid for it the hard way. Don't try to push your painful feelings away; accept and learn from them. Let yourself feel them. Have faith that your feelings and experiences have something to teach you. When you determine what action you need to take or what changes you need to make, put that pain to work. Stress, anger, and other painful feelings can be powerful fuel if you have faith that your pain has a purpose.

Rangers fight through every miserable day of their training and know that each day gets them closer to their goal. We need to be able to hang on through whatever misery we are battling and realize that things will get better each day as we move forward. When my marriage was falling apart and I was enduring my first rotation in Ranger Battalion, I was under extreme duress. I was overwhelmed by feelings that were new to me, and I didn't know how to deal with them. It's very important to learn how to own those kinds of bad feelings when they are happening. Hang on. You'll recognize those feelings and experiences if and when they come again and know that you fought them before and came out winning. When you come out ahead of one bad time, it makes it easier to get through the next one.

You know you've got this, you know how to handle it, and you know it will end. You will continue to push yourself to succeed. You will never quit.

Your perspective will shift if you can just let yourself be in a situation, even if it is the worst situation in the world. If you can start by accepting your circumstances and think, "God, I am here. I am your vessel. What do you need me to do?" your world can open all the way up. Your mission will become clear. You can see and experience everything, take it all in, and begin to take action. I know some people say that we Rangers are not at our best unless someone is shooting at us or throwing hand grenades in our direction. There is some truth to that. Because when you get the opportunity to bring all of your instincts, skill, and faith to bear on a mission, you will focus like a laser. It's an amazing feeling, even when it is dangerous and even when it hurts. Sometimes veterans have a hard time coming back to civilian life in the United States after being immersed in those extreme highs and lows. It's OK, though, you can live like that. God will give you only as much as you can handle. My mom and dad always said that to me, and I've found it to be true.

There are many different ways to serve, and you need to have faith that you will come to know yours. Be thoughtful about your time on this Earth. Do you want to spend it being afraid? Have faith in your journey. Take action. Attack your adversity, even if the obstacle is your own weakness. When I think about the highs and lows in my life so far, I feel as though God was preparing me for Benghazi. Have faith that whatever has happened to you so far is an opportunity to fortify you for the battles ahead as you pursue your mission. All I have ever wanted to do was serve my country. When I tell the story of Benghazi, I think I'm still doing that. May I die at peace with you on the battlefield.

GET AND GIVE HELP

One of my priorities is to honor and support individuals who have sacrificed to protect the United States and their families. Military personnel and first responders can routinely find themselves in tragic and violent situations as part of their work. The unique circumstances of that work can lead to physical and emotional struggles that put people at risk of isolation, despair, and even suicide. Many of these individuals and their families struggle with unmet needs in the months and years following a service-related injury or death. The following organizations are dedicated to honoring and/or assisting veterans and first responders. I encourage you to reach out to them for support if you need it and to consider supporting their work in whatever way you can.

THE UNITED SERVICE ORGANIZATIONS (USO)
www.uso.org

The USO has been providing resources, programs, and entertainment to service members, veterans, and their families since World War II. Today, they provide services at 160 locations around the world. Many people think the USO is a government agency because it works closely with the Department of Defense, but it is a nonprofit charitable corporation chartered by Congress that relies on volunteers and private donations. The USO plays an important role in keeping service members connected to their families and military personnel and their families visited USO centers more than eight million times last year. After September 11, 2012, I was flown from Benghazi to Tripoli and then Germany with not much more than the clothes on my back, and the USO took very good care of me.

THE 14TH HOUR FOUNDATION
www.14hours.org

I helped found the 14th Hour Foundation to raise funds to help veterans, first responders, and military contractor personnel who have served and sacrificed to protect the United States. The funds are disbursed in the form of Honor Grants for unexpected life events that government programs might not cover, such as burial costs, temporary assistance with rent or utility bills, a vehicle repair, or help with college tuition. The 14th Hour also partners with other veteran organizations to provide veteran support services and to increase awareness of veteran-related issues.

THE GLEN DOHERTY MEMORIAL FOUNDATION
www.glendohertyfoundation.org

This foundation honors Bub by assisting current and former special operations professionals with the transition to civilian life by supporting educational and recreational opportunities for service members and their children and families.

THE TYRONE SNOWDEN WOODS
WRESTLING FOUNDATION
www.tyronewoodswrestlingfoundation.org

Tyrone was a champion high school wrestler for Oregon City High School and a state champion of the Oregon State Wrestling Association in 1989. This foundation honors Tyrone by providing financial, educational, and charitable support to high school wrestlers and wrestling programs in Oregon.

GALLANTFEW AND THE RAIDER PROJECT
www.gallantfew.org
www.raiderproject.org

GallantFew offers one-on-one mentoring by a veteran for a veteran, with specific programs for Army Rangers and Marine Corps Raiders, to help create a successful transition to civilian life. GallantFew and the Raider Project have great volunteer networks and partner with other organizations to provide resources and support tailored specifically for veterans by people who know what they are going through. They offer support services ranging from employment and financial assistance through suicide prevention, PTS therapy, and drug addiction treatment to other programs promoting physical and spiritual fitness.

SPECIAL OPERATIONS WOUNDED WARRIORS
www.sowwcharity.com

Special Operations Wounded Warriors assists active duty and veteran members of all US special ops forces with charitable outdoor events, family retreats, and therapeutic treatments. It particularly recognizes the sacrifice of those who have sustained wounds in service and offer strength, comfort, and aid for their rehabilitation.

SPORTSMEN FOR WARRIORS
www.sportsmenforwarriors.org

Sportsmen for Warriors provides life-enhancing support through educational, training, and enrichment opportunities for military, veteran, and first responder men and women and their families. It offers unique recreational opportunities in the outdoors that help warriors connect with one another and bridge the gap between military leadership skills and civilian job requirements.

ACKNOWLEDGMENTS

'm still amazed that I was given the opportunity to write a book about overcoming adversity utilizing my own experiences. I wouldn't have had this opportunity if I hadn't watched and learned from others, whether being successful or failing miserably. There are many people who have helped me, and I want to acknowledge them here.

Thank you to Kate Hartson and everyone at Center Street for believing in *The Ranger Way*. I am grateful to Richard Abate at 3 Arts Entertainment for his expertise, friendship, and guidance throughout this project as well as the book that started this freight train: *13 Hours: The Inside Account of What Really Happened in Benghazi*. Thanks are due to Mitchell Zuckoff for helping me and my fellow GRS operators write *13 Hours* and for becoming a trusted confidant whom I could call with questions any time day or night. This project was more emotionally difficult for me than *13 Hours* and I am grateful to Melissa Moore for helping me write *The Ranger Way* and for being patient with me during the process. Many thanks to my GRS team for standing together, not only during the attacks in Benghazi but also as we moved through unfamiliar territory in the public eye. Thanks to Erwin Stoff and Michael Bay, who etched our story in Hollywood history and treated me and my teammates with respect, honor, and honesty. I call Pablo Schreiber a friend to this day, and I'm grateful to him for working his tail off on set to bring Tanto to life accurately on the big screen and upholding the Ranger standard of giving one hundred percent and then some. I am lucky to have Judy Landreth Wilkinson's expertise, enthusiasm, and friendship as I navigate the new professional path God has set me on.

Thank you to my former 2nd Battalion, 75th Ranger Regiment, CSM Peter Rothke, who epitomized what I believed the 75th Ranger Regiment embodies: toughness, honor, loyalty, and never-quit attitude. Yes, CSM, I did owe you more time. Thank you to one 2nd Battalion, 75th Ranger Regiment, Tabbed Spec 4 whom I saw as a mentor and looked up to as I was trying to earn my Ranger SFC: Keith Bach. I was lucky to play football at Dixie Junior College for Coach Greg Croshaw, whom I saw bring so many different personalities together, utilizing the essence of brotherhood and teamwork to put together a powerhouse junior college football team.

Many thanks are due to my longtime friend Matt Selcke: I was lucky to grow up with you, play high school and college football with you, and serve in the 75th Ranger Regiment by your side. Matt, you literally saved my life, and I know you would be there for me even if I called you today. I love you, brother. Thank you to Ranger SSG Alex Saenz, my man Guapo: you took care of me when I came back through Basic, you took care of me at Ranger BN and on multiple deployments to Afghanistan. I repaid you with misery. I apologize and want you to know that I wouldn't have made it through Benghazi without you and the example of your unselfish conduct through our many years of friendship and operations together.

Thank you to my brother, Mike: I love you and still remember our fights growing up and also how proud I always was to call you my brother. Thank you to my sister, Jamie, still the smartest of all three of us: I know you have struggled, but you always move forward and I love you for your strength. I love and miss my Grandpa Joaquin and and Grandma Rose Garcia, who taught me that hard work and perseverance are a necessity in life if you want to be successful; that handouts are not acceptable; and that the best safety net in life is a job. Thank you, most of all, to my mother and father, Rita and Jim Paronto: You showed me love, kindness, and discipline. You taught me how to endure failure and then to use that failure and a fire to work my ass off so I would never fail again. You taught me that hard work always pays off and that if you start something, you finish it. Dad, you are my hero; you gave me confidence just by showing me how to look into a man's eye when shaking his hand, and you showed me how to be patient. Mom, you gave me a lot of fire, which I have needed to accomplish everything I have been lucky enough to do. I love you guys immensely.

There are many people I can't name here, but I want to acknowledge my Blackwater Security brothers, who made things happen in Iraq when the US State Department couldn't find its way out of a room with one door, and then stood in the line of fire to ensure that those same US State Department officials were able to make it home safely. To all those who have served and are still serving with the 75th Ranger Regiment: We may not have always gotten the accolades or recognition as other SOCOM units, but know that without the 75th, the Global War on Terror and following combat operations would not have been successful. God bless you all.

—Kris "Tanto" Paronto

ABOUT THE AUTHOR

KRIS "TANTO" PARONTO is a former Army Ranger from 2nd Battalion, 75th Ranger Regiment, and private security contractor who has deployed throughout South America, Central America, the Middle East, and North Africa. He has worked with the US government's Global Response Staff, the US State Department Diplomatic Security High Threat Protection Pro-

Barry Morgenstein Photography

gram, and Blackwater Security Consulting conducting low-profile security in high-threat environments throughout the world. He is the coauthor of the book *13 Hours: The Inside Account of What Really Happened in Benghazi*, describing his experience responding to the 2012 terrorist attack on the US Special Mission in Benghazi, Libya, with Mitchell Zuckoff and the five surviving security team members. Tanto has started his own Tactical Training company along with Laurence "OD" Greene called Battleline Tactical Training. He is a brand ambassador for Maxim Defense Industries, Thaddea, and VertX and is a featured writer for national publications. Tanto speaks regularly throughout the United States on leadership, faith, and motivation. He lives in Omaha, Nebraska.